Thoughts for Searchers

Seeking to Understand Life:

Reflections of

Imam W. Deen Mohammed

Edited by

Ronald B. Shaheed

Thoughts for Searchers Seeking to Understand Life: Reflections of Imam W. Deen Mohammed

Edited & Published by Ronald B. Shaheed

Copyright 2012

ISBN 978-0-615-70777-8

Thoughts for Searchers

CONTENTS

What Others Said About Imam W. Deen Mohammed

"Wallace Deen Muhammed is a dreamer, but he is a dreamer-cum-realist, and gentle, sensitive, and self-effacing. History may yet prove him to be one of the most astute religious leaders of this age, regardless of communion. A lifelong student of Islam, fluent in Arabic, and well conversant with the nuances of Qur'anic ideology and its institutionalized projections, Wallace is no less a keen and perceptive observer of the American scene. Therein lies his potential for achievement and service to Islam." C. Eric Lincoln, "The Muslim Mission in the Context of American Social History", *African-American Religion: Interpretive Essays in History and Culture*, T. E. Fulop & A. J. Raboteau, Routledge, New York, NY, 1997, p. 288.

****

"Among the speakers came Imam Wallace D. Muhammed, reciting Qur'anic verses of peace in Arabic and English. An ally of Malcolm X in his youth, Muhammed had gone on to reform his own father's sectarian Nation of Islam. In a book interview, he once had expressed to me his long-term ambition for American Muslims to help reconcile world Islam with democracy. I considered Muhammed the nation's most underappreciated religious figure in the twentieth century, but here he was preaching unnoticed to the incoming Clintons..." Taylor Branch (Pulitzer Prize-winning author of *America in the King Years*), *The Clinton Tapes: Wrestling History with the President*, Simon & Schuster, New York, NY, 2009, p. 24.

****

"Militant Muslims remain a fractious minority who stress the confrontational aspect of monotheistic faith. Other Muslims demur. Notable amongst them is the voice of Imam W. D. Mohammed...An African-American Muslim leader; he has provided guidance to millions of his co-religionists who had previously defined Islam by race as much as by creed. Since the 1960s he has led them into mainstream Islam and also into mainstream America. Imam Mohammed contests that the Qur'an provides a staging ground for apocalyptic warfare. For him the Qur'an does require *jihad*, but it is not *jihad* as all-out war. It is *jihad* as an eternal battle between good and evil. The highest temporal pursuit for Muslims, in his view, is to be pragmatic citizens of a twenty-first-century global community. Deeply grounded in a Qur'anic world-view, Imam Mohammed remains open to engagement with non-Muslims. He seeks allies in a larger war against poverty, racism, and environmental degradation. He values a world at peace where the true *jihad* is for justice, not armed conflict motivated by hatred or displayed as terror." Bruce Lawrence, *The Qur'an: A Biography*, Atlantic Monthly Press, New York, 2006, pp. 16-17.

****

"We have had many meetings with our Muslim friends. What characterizes these gatherings above all is the presence of God which one notices when they pray, and which gives much hope. I saw this hope become a reality in the Malcolm Shabazz Mosque in Harlem (USA) six years ago when I was invited to explain my Christian experience to 3,000 African-American Muslims. Their welcome, beginning with that of their leader, Imam W. D. Mohammed, was so warm, sincere and enthusiastic that it led us to great expectations for the future. I returned three years ago to the United States, to Washington, to make a presentation about our working together before a large convention of 7,000 Christians and Muslims. In an atmosphere of the greatest elation and accompanied by endless applause we exchanged a sincere embrace, promising each other we would continue our journey in the fullest union possible and spread it to others." Chiara Lubich (leader of the International Focolare Movement), *Chiara Lubich: The Essential Writings*, New City Press, Hyde Park, NY, 2007, p. 345.

****

"I have followed Imam W. Deen Mohammed's work for nearly 20 years and I am a long admirer of his keen mind and dedication, but most of all his spiritual growth. When he had an opportunity to erect and dedicate a giant ego for himself, he refused. Instead of training the spotlight on the illusion of fame, he decided to become an example of his true self, and let G_d's light shine from within. The African-American Community, more than ever, needs a moral compass. We have surrendered to the ego of a lost leadership. Imam W. Deen Mohammed has been one of the few who has continually provided moral leadership that possesses a creative vision. He is a beacon of light, follow him."

Thoughts for Searchers

Tony Brown, Journalist, Host, *Tony Brown's Journal, A Look at W. Deen Mohammed, Muslim American Spokesman for Human Salvation,* a Ministry of W. Deen Mohammed Publication, 1993, Calumet City, IL, p. 6.

****

"Imam W. Deen Mohammed is one of the most enlightened religious leaders in our world today. He played a major role in bringing American Muslims into the mainstream of religious life in the U.S.A. He is a pioneer in developing good relations between Muslims and Jews in America which was dramatized by our historic pulpit exchange in Washington and Chicago in 1978. I am deeply impressed by his spiritual leadership and pray for G_d's blessings upon his good work." Joshua O. Haberman, Senior Rabbi Emeritus, Washington Hebrew Congregation, July 1992, *A Look at W. Deen Mohammed, Muslim American Spokesman for Human Salvation,* a Ministry of W. Deen Mohammed Publication, 1993, Calumet City, IL, p. 4.

****

"I have known Imam W. Deen Mohammed since 1966. I have always known him to be a spiritual man who like myself, has been quick to make a stand for what he truly believed, even when it caused him to be 'exiled' from his family and the Muslim community as we knew it in the 60s and early 70s. Without faltering, he led the American Muslim Community through a difficult time after the death of the Honorable Elijah Muhammed. Throughout that difficult period he exhibited patience, humility and forbearance and a clear vision of Al-Islam...He has worked hard to better relations between Muslims and people of other religions in order to achieve a peaceful coexistence here and in other parts of the world. He has helped Americans to understand what the true religion of Islam is about and sought to neutralize the negative overtones given to Muslims and our religion through the media. He has brought the American Muslim community much closer to other Islamic communities throughout the world. He is highly respected in all Islamic societies. I applaud Imam W. Deen Mohammed for all his good works and all that he continues to do to promote the cause of Allah...We should pray every day for Allah to bless this man and keep him safe and strong in his mission. It is truly a blessing from Allah that he is with us." Muhammed Ali, humanitarian and three time World

Thoughts for Searchers

Heavyweight Boxing Champion, *A Look at W. Deen Mohammed, Muslim American Spokesman for Human Salvation,* a Ministry of W. Deen Mohammed Publication, 1993, Calumet City, IL, p.10.

****

"Despite our sharing of existential space with almost 6 billion human beings, in actual fact we know and relate to only a very few of them during our lives. Not so for people like the imam, who grew up as the son of a famous man whose thoughts and actions affected the lives and times of thousands of Americans and others worldwide. Like his father, Warith Deen believed deeply in the capacity and capability of the African American and that their moral and social transformation was imperative. Through words and deeds, he so inspired countless young and old people all over the world that they came to consider him a leader, a mentor, and a friend for life…Although the imam has answered G_d's call, his spirit will continue to affect many of us. He started with what he knew and built on what he had. This was his message, and American students of religious thought and activism will hopefully visit his path and share his findings. Thank G_d Almighty for granting life and good health to this man. He lived well, with love and mercy for all and with dreams and hopes for justice everywhere." Dr. Sulayman S. Nyang, Howard University, Washington, DC, "The Transformer-in-Chief", *Islamic Horizons Magazine,* November/December 2008, pp. 16-18.

****

"The Sufis say: 'The true sage belongs to his era.' And of the many gifts given to Imam WDM by G_d, perhaps the most obvious and beneficial one was the Imam's profound understanding of the *principles* of religion, and his adeptness at *intelligently applying* those Islamic principles in a socially and culturally appropriate manner befitting the everyday lives of his North American followers. While carefully respecting sound, traditional jurisprudential methodologies of the Islamic religion, and the collective religious history and time-honored scholarship of classical Islam, he promulgated creative ideas and dynamic teachings across many domains of human endeavor, including theology, law, spirituality and even ethics and aesthetics, that together articulated a vision for a quintessentially 'American

Thoughts for Searchers

Muslim' cultural identity. And he did all of this before anyone else, with quiet strength and unending humility-a true sage indeed." Azhur Usman, "...An Apology", *Islamic Horizons Magazine*, November/December 2008, p. 28.

****

"The genius of Imam W. D. was that he single-handedly moved the African American community toward identifying with pluralist American identity while moving away from Black Nationalist Islam. Today, millions of African American Muslims are comfortable with being as strongly American as they are being devout Muslims, demonstrating the two are not incompatible. This achievement is due entirely to Imam W. D." Akbar Ahmed, *Journey into America: The Challenge of Islam*, Brookings Institution Press, Washington, D.C., 2010, p. 174.

Preface

He has been called, "America's Imam", but for 33 years he was simply, Imam W. Deen Mohammed, to his devoted students and followers many of whom were the harvest of the followers his father, the Honorable Elijah Mohammed, led in the Nation of Islam from 1933-1975. I, initially, was a devoted follower of his father but was among the exuberant proto-Islamic mass of "Black Muslims" who, in 1975, followed Imam W. Deen Mohammed onto the path of classical Islam that was established by Muhammed, the Prophet (prayers and the peace be on him), more than 1,400 years ago.

No one in my lifetime has done more to promote human excellence, decency and peace among people of all races, faiths, etc. than Imam W. Deen Mohammed. G_d blessed me to travel with him across the United States of America as he appealed to the vibrant minds of America's college and university students to take up the work of promoting human enlightenment and progress here in America and throughout the world.

Additionally, I was blessed to travel with him to Rome, Italy and the Vatican on several occasions as he worked to promote interfaith cooperation and understanding with Catholics and other Christians of the world. He permitted me to accompany him (in a delegation) to Saudi Arabia, where he was the guest of the ruler, King Fahd bin Abdul Aziz in 1995 and to Palestine (Jerusalem, Gaza, Jericho, Bethlehem, Hebron, etc.) to dialogue with the Palestinian people and to meet with President Yassir Arafat in 1996. Imam W. Deen Mohammed also sent me to Germany in 2003 to represent him at a weeklong European youth camp attended by young adults between the ages of 18 and 25 from quite a number of European nations. In all of these experiences I observed and met people who expressed great love and abiding respect for America's Imam.

A few months before his passing, Imam W. Deen Mohammed met with representatives of the Presbyterian Church USA to establish a four year dialogue between his associates and the Presbyterian Church USA. This dialogue was initiated one month after his passing in October 2008 in Chicago, IL and was conducted (with the involvement of Presbyterians and Muslim associates of Imam Mohammed) over the next four years in Chicago, IL, Louisville, KY, Indianapolis, IN, Atlanta, GA, St. Louis, MO, Philadelphia, PA,

Thoughts for Searchers

Oakland, CA and Charlotte, NC.

About a year prior to his passing Imam Mohammed suggested the title for this book, *Thoughts for Searchers*. He said there were people of elevated thinking that would appreciate a compilation of some of his intimate thoughts on a variety of subjects. As I compiled and edited this material I certainly gained an intense, renewed appreciation for Imam W. Deen Mohammed's "thoughts". I pray that you will too.

Ronald Bilal Shaheed

Milwaukee, 2012

1

Logic for All People

We may have a truth in America, or the United States, that might not hold up, or it might not be true in China. But in al-Islam whatever we believe in is supposed to hold up everywhere. No matter where you go it is supposed to stand up and appeal to the logic of all people and it is supposed to stand up in their good senses. When you communicate with each other, especially when you are serious, be sure that what you are saying can stand up in the good senses of the person you are talking to.

Man, when he had to survive, before civilization, or before the development of towns and conveniences for people living together in big numbers, he was living in a natural environment and seeking his means of support for his life in that natural environment. Now, we know how valuable the natural environment is to the development of human beings in community and society, because without that support we wouldn't have gotten to science and education or science and industry. The first life was supported by the natural environment and this is the man born of the earth or born of the ground.

But once community starts to develop, community takes man's attention from the natural environment and man then is formed inside of the community life. He's not formed inside of the natural environment. He's formed inside of community life. Consequently, the man born of a woman has to have more knowledge of life in community.

So the teaching changes from a man in a natural, material situation or environment where nature in its raw picture is supporting him. Now, he is a product of togetherness or a product of society, itself, living together with others and benefitting from the things that were brought from the natural environment and put into the town environment, or the city environment, etc. So, he doesn't go out to get these things anymore. Originally, the husband had to go out to get those things that he needed to support his family's life. But, now, he doesn't have to go out there anymore. Those things are brought by others, farmers and whatever. They are brought by others and when he gets them they are already finished. So he doesn't have to leave the town; like a baby doesn't have to leave or get out of his mother's womb, out of her body, to get all that he needs to become complete as a physical life.

Cities as women

Now, here is a man living in his town or city life and in the Bible all of these towns or big cities are given female names, women's names, and they all are charged with sinning or going astray from G_d's way. So, they are wicked women. They are seen as bad women. And I agree, that most of the clusters that we find in these big cities, people all clustered together, they are bad mothers.

It takes a village to raise a child

In Africa, in the little towns, you could trust the raising of your child to the whole town. They say, Africans say, "It takes a whole village to raise a child". Well, I don't want the whole city raising my child! Good G_d Almighty!

Jesus was born of a woman, but he was born of a pure woman. No man touched her. She was not supported by man. She was supported, directly, by G_d. The Spirit that went into her was not the spirit of man. It was the Spirit of G_d and it produced a son born of the Spirit of G_d; Jesus Christ, a word and a Spirit from G_d.

Straining the Mind for Understanding

It is called the ganglia that, that comes from the spine to the brain and goes back down, back into the system, back into the whole body. It comes into the conscious, sometimes; maybe no time. But if it comes into the conscious then the brain sees what it couldn't see before. It's sometimes called the sixth sense. You might call it intuitive insight. So it goes from the ganglia to the forebrain, the forefront. And most of the time it comes there but it doesn't register in the conscious. It goes back and forth. It comes from the ganglia to the forebrain. It goes back from the forebrain, the lobe in the front, back to the back brain, the hemisphere in the back and then down to the ganglia.

Going up the mountain and coming back down

For example, you've got some basic or general understanding of a matter or idea that you're trying to develop or arrive at and you need to perceive or show where this general matter is taking you or where it is trying to go. Where it's trying to go should be the topic or caption for the whole structure and it's proceeding to where? It's proceeding to the top. That's the mountain. It's trying to get to the top of the mountain. And then, once you're at the top of the mountain, if you find the right thing, it should be applicable all down below. So that's going up the mountain and coming back down with what you achieved, with what you perceived to be the life or the benefit for those living in community life, whether Christian or Muslim.

Thoughts for Searchers

When we do the ritual washing for prayer, or the wudu', we take water into our hands and then bring it forward (from the base of the head to the front) and then we bring it back down. Really, this is the mountain. The head is symbolic of the mountain. Actually, the mountain is just speaking of the human body. So, at the base of the skull are the ganglia and this is where thoughts form that have a direction and a conclusion. They start there (at the base of the skull) and they go up to the conscious (in the front). The front, or the face, is consciousness.

"Unless they bear fruit…"

So they come out and struggle for development and they reach consciousness and then when you go back down (to the base of the skull) you're applying it to the ganglia, or to the ignorant people. You have to bring it forward and pull it back down where it started. It started in the darkness. Now, you're going to bring light to the darkness. It is now concluded.

They start from the base, or from generalities, and they have a direction to become fruitful. They want to get to the top, because at the top is where they become fruitful. Now they're bearing fruit. So now they take the fruit and bring the fruit down to earth where people can benefit from it. And for the straining in the mind to understand, they call it cognition. Once cognition reaches the top (the front of the face, or consciousness) you now have fruition and it's going to bear fruit. Now, take it back down to the people.

So Jesus said, "Unless they bear fruit…" And they think it means out there fishing people in and doing other things, etc. No, it means for your own mind, the straining of your mind to understand G_d's world that He created so you can establish yourself in it, be successful and lead mankind the way Allah wants them to be led on this planet earth. That's the big picture.

Body inherits the past

I don't think it is known where it comes from, but I think insight brought Muhammed, the Prophet, and his followers and many people over the world to understand what it comes from. It's rested in the body and the body has inherited the past. Every person that lived before that had anything to do with that person, everybody in the genetic line of that person, all of that information can come to that person. And it's in the body. It's in the genes. It's in the body; and the ganglia are the nerve lines connecting to the brain.

Come back to G_d

So it can come from there up into the brain and the brain can release it to the conscious if the person is conditioned to bring it out. And you know that's what khaleefah is. Khaleefah means, literally, "that that is behind you". Khalfan means, "Behind you". If I say, "Huwa khalfan", it means, "He is behind me". Consequently, khaleefah means, "That, that is behind you in time, or, in your genetic line". So G_d made the khaleefah and G_d made Adam khaleefah. It means that He made Adam (man, the human being) to register his past in his conscious. And if he registers his past in his conscious, eventually, he's going to come back to G_d. He's going to realize that in his past there was nothing that was under his control. "All of this is under the control of my Creator" and he gives the credit to G_d. And then he becomes khaleefah if he has the desire to release that, to share that with people, like Imam Warith Deen Mohammed. But if he has no interest to give to people he'll never register it in his conscious. It will never register on his conscious. And even if he has the desire, it's still the Will of G_d. The right things have to happen to bring it to the conscious and don't think you can do it without G_d's personal help. You have to prove yourself, first. When you prove yourself then G_d's personal help will come to you.

Khaleefah (Adam) a common possession of all people

So Khaleefah is a common possession of all people (Adam). Adam is a part of all people and khaleefah is a common possession of all people. G_d in the Qur'an says He made you, "Khulifah in the earth". That's the plural of khaleefah. He made you khaleefahs in the earth and then He says He also made you inheritors in the earth. So you have the khaleefah property in your nature, in your creation. But He also made you inheritors. You can inherit that property. You are the inheritor of that property. So it's a common nature and common property and all people have it.

And that's the Christ nature, too. But the Christ nature is above this possession or form. What I'm talking about is a form or property of the human form and

Jesus Christ is on a level above that in the Ascension, or Miraj. He is on a level above that, with John. And that's to say that on his level (the second level of heaven) the urge is to express it. Whereas, on the Adam level (the first level of heaven) the urge is just to benefit from it, unconsciously.

The life and possibilities for the common people

And Prophet John, peace be on all of the prophets, he's on the same level with Jesus Christ because his urge, too, was to express it. But Jesus Christ was raised in a religious environment. John, the Baptist, was a desert man, so he couldn't speak well. But he was expressing it, too. "You'd better get right! You'd better get right! The time is at hand!" He knew that much. It's beautiful and it's saying what is the life and possibilities of the common people; for the common people, everybody. But only a few manage to have it expressed in their nature, or for them.

No History without G_d

When you read al-Fatiha (the first chapter of Qur'an) and come to understand it you will know that al-Fatiha helps us to understand why the stories of the people of 'Ad and any other people are in the Qur'an. It is because Allah is Lord of all people. He cares about all the worlds and they could not have any history without G_d. We could not have history without G_d. We could not have this nation, nor have our form of government without revelation from G_d. We could not have this beautiful form of government we have if the Qur'an had not come. There was no government like we have in this United States before the Qur'an. The Christians were not able to establish a government like this before the Qur'an. It was the Qur'an that guided the founding fathers to conceive what was in their own book, the Bible, and they used the Qur'an to arrive at the logic supporting this philosophy called American democracy.

It is said that the first president, George Washington, had knowledge of Qur'an. James Madison was known to have spoken highly of the Qur'an, Muhammed, the Prophet and al-Islam. So those people back there that formed this idea we call American Democracy were acquainted with Muhammed, the Prophet, and the Qur'an; and they definitely were inspired by Muhammed and guided by the knowledge that G_d gave him to form the ideas supporting the Constitution of the United States of America. This I'm convinced of and I have no doubts at all about it.

Built for all people

The Masons are a secret order. Many of our presidents were Shriners and Masons and when you look at the symbols that they have or that they show more than any other, what are they? They are universal signs, the compass and square. But where is the compass and square? Do you know where the compass and square is in al Islam? When you make Hajj (Pilgrimage) you make circles around a square and it's a universal sign, a universal place for all mankind.

And the house that was built there, Allah says in our Holy Book, it was built for all people, not just one people, not for Arabs only. The Qur'an says, "Buneyal len nas, built for all mankind". That's in Qur'an. I'm giving you G_d's Word. It's a house, the oldest of houses, the most ancient of houses, built for all people. And I bet some of you thought it was built for Allah, for G_d. Solomon, the Prophet Sulaiman (in Al Islam) long before Muhammed and before the Qur'an was revealed, it (the Bible) says he built a house and he said, "G_d, I know this house can't house You. Not even the heaven of heavens is big enough to house you".

People are one family

Prophets long before Muhammed knew that you could not house G_d. So it (Ka'bah) is not a house for G_d. Allah is not in that house. That is a house symbolically saying that all people came from one family. That is all it says. Everybody is to go to that one house and that is to say that all people came from one family; the family of the first man and woman, Adam and his wife; the first human beings. It says that people are one family. That is what the house says. In al-Islam we have to accept that and it is the fifth pillar of our religion, Hajj.

Logic of all people

And how do you write five in Arabic? Five in Arabic is a circle, which means complete. And a circle means eternally without an end, because if you write a line you are going to come to an end unless you curve that straight line to make a circle. Eventually, you are going to come to the end of the straight line. But a circle, you can do it forever. You can go in a circle forever. But, we don't want you circling forever. We just want you to circle seven times around the Ka'bah. We just want you to understand that these things have deep meaning and men have used these things to address other things that they believe in. It appeals to the universal truths that they believe in, things that hold up everywhere. We may have a truth in America or the United States that might not hold up or it might not be true in China. But in al-Islam whatever we believe in is supposed to hold up everywhere. No matter where you go it is supposed to stand up and appeal to the logic of all people; and it is supposed to stand up in their good senses.

When you communicate with each other, especially when you are serious, be sure that what you are saying can stand up in the good senses of the person you are talking to. Don't waste time with foolishness when you are trying to be serious. When you're serious be serious and be like the wise; even your joke is to be serious. The wise man if he makes jokes, his jokes are wisdom; that is, if he is serious.

The Beauty of Life

Life is beautiful. Even the worst things we see we don't perceive them correctly, most of us. The environment we live in of people negatively influences the way we see things. So here you're living in an environment in one area of the world and winter is ugly and cold. In another area of the world winter is beautiful; cool, or chilly, but beautiful.

Winter anywhere is beautiful. All you have to do is look at one snowflake under the microscope or under a magnifier and you have enough to warm you up. Look at the beauty in the dust that does not show its beauty. You have to look very closely. G_d says in the Qur'an He spread the earth out like a carpet. Now even if you're flying over the sands of Saudi Arabia and you look down it looks like a carpet. That beautiful sand looks like a carpet. And when you're flying over the jungle if you're high enough it doesn't look like you're looking down on trees. It looks like you're looking down on a carpet, because they come so much together when you're far away until actually it looks like it's covered with green. That is some deep carpet. Man loves grain, so there are long stretches of grass where they grow wheat and other grasses, rye, etc.; miles and miles. It looks like a beautiful green carpet. Then the grass is taken and mown, so it really looks, close up, like a carpet.

Beauty in nature's violence

Layers of beauty, the Lord has made this creation in layers of beauty. In G_d's world even violence is beautiful. You see the way a hawk or eagle comes swooping down. It is like a theater and you can just watch it. If you don't put your mind on the victim you will really enjoy it. That is some artful stuff they're doing there. So G_d has always left something beautiful in whatever He presents. He leaves something beautiful to tell you this is happening but this is not the general rule or pattern. What you should be seeing is the beauty that is prevalent in everything, even death. The dead thing looks so restful.

Don't just look at the outer picture

The ice that we don't like that makes the winter cold they put it in the glass to pour champagne or soft drink over it and look how pretty it looks. Crystallization, they have exploited it all the way, as much as they could, to make beautiful China or crystal glass ware. But the artist he looks at it very close up, with a magnifying glass and he finds inspiration in the crystallization. He ends up making a masterpiece of art just copying the crystallization in the material. And colors, too, crystals, they form beautiful colors. They all are not clear, not transparent. Some of them are colored and very beautiful. So you go in the redwood forest, called the Petrified Forest, in California and you find some of the beautiful pieces of petrified wood where crystals have formed and colors have formed in such beautiful patterns. Now look how they died. They died beautiful, didn't they? So it is speaking to man's spirit. Don't just look at the outer picture, look into it.

Actors on a stage

We're nothing but pieces in the puzzle, actors on the stage, given a role to play. We're not our own creator. We didn't make ourselves. And if it's for you, you can't escape it. You'll be going down a road that's not even in the world that has been designed for you. But when it's time for you to come out, you're going to come out of that world and you're going to get on the road to the destiny G_d created you for.

More to names than we think

Every human being whether they are aware of it or not, have a role that is prepared for them. There's a role prepared for them and sometimes it's not major at all, very minor. It has no real meaning in man's world. It has no presence, no meaning in man's world. But what G_d has designed for one of us He designed for all of us. If He designed it for one, it's designed for all. Yes, you had to be what you are. You couldn't be anything different. It's the same for all of us. It's in G_d's plan and I don't believe anybody receives a name without it being in G_d's plan that they be named that. If his name is "Dog", or "Hyena", I don't care what his name is, that name had to be approved by Allah, by G_d, the Creator, before that name could be accepted in his life. If that name isn't to be his it is not going to be his, no matter what it is. So there is more to names than we think, much more.

I've done it, studied for many years now, at least for longer than my life as a leader. I have studied for more than half of my life as the leader how names influence the outcome of the person that has that name. Now, sometimes the person can defeat the influence of the name and become the opposite of it, whether good or bad; become the opposite of that name. But that name was the cause of that person making the change. So we can't name anything and I guess I always knew that. I never wanted the power to name. Whatever my wife wanted I let her do, even though I didn't agree with it. I wouldn't give a name unless she asked me to give names. If my wife asked, "Can you give me some names", I would never give her just one name. I would give her several for her to select one from it. That was just my nature. It had nothing to do with me fearing to do that; that Allah wouldn't approve of it or something like that. Allah didn't come into the picture at all. It was just my spirit, just my nature and spirit that I didn't want to name a human being. I thought the mother should be the one to do it; or, I'd give her help; help her select a name.

Conditions for Coming into Heaven

The Bible says, or G_d in the Bible says, "No one has ascended to heaven except he who was in heaven already". We are to understand that also in this way: that the condition for you coming into heaven is inherent. Whatever takes you to heaven is already in your makeup, inborn. You are born with it. It is part of your makeup. It is your property as a creature, as a human being. It is your property that you're born with that takes you to heaven, that utility or whatever we want to call it that takes you to heaven. So you had it before you were formed in the earth. If it is inherent you had it before you were formed in the earth, because all of us are formed in our mothers' stomachs. Somebody told me, trying to be smart, to show that they know something, "Brother Imam, we're not formed in our mother's stomach. We're formed in..." and they gave the scientific language. But I don't care what you are formed in, my mother's stomach grew when my little brother was coming into this world and I saw her stomach get bigger and bigger to accommodate my brother's body growing in her.

So G_d is not talking to us through the intelligence or the knowledge of a few scientists or people. He's talking to us addressing, appealing, to our common sense. And our common sense says, children, babies, grow in their mothers and are delivered from their mother's stomachs. So that is the language G_d uses. If He uses the language that science uses He will miss most of the people. And some of them can't understand anything else but the baby is growing in mama's stomach. So no matter what is inside the stomach, the stomach is the outer envelope and it is definitely in there. It is in a shroud or a seal, the water bag. But the water bag is in the stomach and the stomach expands to accommodate the baby.

Possibilities in your mind, soul and heart

So what I understand the two books (Bible and Qur'an) to be saying is that we shouldn't look outside of the human life into some realms of the unknown, like most people are conditioned to do in religion, for a situation to achieve our utmost as a human being with the freedom that G_d created for us. That marvelous experience where you are going to be transformed into a higher life and for a higher purpose will not take place if you don't believe that the possibilities are there in your mind, your soul, your heart. If you think that something has to come from up there so it can assist you, you are never going to make it. That is what both the Bible and Qur'an are telling us.

Respect your five senses

Prophet Muhammed, the prayers and the peace be upon him, said, "If a river or stream of water would pass by and you would wash in that water five times a day would there be any impurities left?" His followers said, "No". So he was telling them, "Don't forget your five senses when you're cleaning yourself in wudu' (ritual washing) before prayer (five times a day). He was telling them in a wise way, "Respect your five senses, because here is a stream that comes and you wash in it five times and no more impurities are left". It doesn't mean five times, literally. It means we're washing using our five senses. And they understood him. He was speaking to the wise. They said, "No impurities will be left if we use our five senses".

G_d is the best of Creators

G_d wants us to be creators. We hear the West talking about creators, "Man creating this, man creating that. We want people with creativity to work in this plant," and they will give you a special room if you qualify. If they think you have a brain that you can really create for their company they will give you a special room and you will sit in a very comfortable environment and read whatever you want. You can write whatever comes into your mind. They will play the best music for you to listen to quietly and they will not to disturb you, except just to soothe your mind and soul while you work for them. That is what the big money people will do. That shows you how much they think of creation and people creating. They believe you can become creators. G_d, when He says, "G_d Ahsanu khaalqeen, G_d is the best and most beautiful of the creators", well, who are the other creators He's mentioning? He didn't say one. He says He is the best of the creators. So He's saying there are other creators. Who are they?

"Nothing is more productive than the human brain"

Angels never created anything, that's not their job. Their job is just to serve G_d, keep creation like He made it and to punish those who take it out of the plan He wants it in. Those are angels. So who is He talking about? He's talking about man and when we say man we mean woman, too. It is talking about the human intellect. That's exactly what He's talking about.

Muhammed said of the human intellect, "G_d never created anything more useful and productive than the human brain". That's what Muhammed, the Prophet, said and it's obvious all these things are the result of our brains. Muhammed told us and we know it's the truth, "Nothing is more productive than the human brain". Allah created the best thing, the human brain.

Knowledge locked up in creation to be discovered

And when you read the story of mankind, the beginning of our fathers, our family of human beings with Adam, G_d is introducing him as an intellect, not as a spiritual spook or something. He's an intellect, a wise brain. G_d made a creature with a wise, useful mind, brain, and then gave him the world so that he can get the benefits of it; so that he can become very productive and make his life better on earth by using the wonderful things that G_d has locked up. Yes, they are locked up. Our knowledge and study has to bring them out. They are locked up in His creation.

"Read in the Name of Your Lord Who Created"

G_d began the first revelation to Muhammed, the Prophet, with the words, "Read in the name of your Lord Who created..." Muhammed wasn't just hearing these words, he was being educated. His mind was being opened up to the light of just how man becomes a wonderful community or established in beautiful way and it begins with creation, man's own form. G_d created you, formed you to have this social nature and if you appreciate this social nature then you will not only know G_d as your Creator, or as the One Who helped you develop your form or get your form up into existence. But you will know G_d as a kind and generous G_d, because your wealth is going to increase as your social life improves. You are going to be rewarded because of your social appreciation for your social life. You are going to be rewarded with an abundance of things, of all kinds of wonderful things. Isn't that true?

Needs are social more than anything else

So when G_d says (in the first part of the revelation to Muhammed), "Read in the name of your Lord Who created," it connects you with creation and then connects you with your needs as a creation. You are creation. What are your needs? Your needs are social more than anything else. The social need is what requisitions more than anything else. We have all of this because of our social needs. You just look around at the buildings, etc., whatever it is it is because of our social needs that we have all of this. If we wanted nothing but the spiritual we would be up on top of a hill somewhere levitating, meditating, or something. We wouldn't need all of these structures if we didn't want anything but spiritual life. Those people who don't want anything but spiritual life they don't build houses, roads, and all of these things to take care of human beings living in social groups.

So what did G_d do? He took Muhammed and connected him with the created world. Then, He showed him in this created world, "What is more important for you, Muhammed, is your social nature" and aren't we called brothers and sisters? That is identifying the social bonds, isn't it? That is what it is talking about, social bonds. We are bonded so importantly together, we call ourselves brothers and sisters, like the children of two parents, male and female, putting emphasis on our social grouping or social bonds. And it says because of man giving attention to his social nature man came into knowledge, sciences, and higher education, etc.

Logic for All People

First five verses of revelation (Qur'an) because of man's five senses

All of this is communicated to Muhammed in these first few verses and they are five. The first group is five. It is no accident. You have five senses and you are a complete life because you have five senses. You can feel, you can hear, you can see, you can smell, you can taste, and the objective sciences or the pure sciences they trust nothing but the five senses.

Empirical science comes via the five senses

You who went to college and studied, in the first year maybe you didn't learn anything. But if you stay there after that year they are going to start teaching you something; and I'm sure they taught you, maybe in the first year, the expression, "Empirical sciences," those sciences that are trusted to nothing but the five senses. You know I'm correct. If my five senses can't witness it, it doesn't exist for the empirical sciences or the objective sciences.

Upon what the five senses can perceive or know reasoning and logic come into play and then you can arrive at beliefs that they call theories, axioms, and postulates, whatever. All of these things you arrive at are not facts in themselves. But the five senses pointed you in that direction from studying, observing these things. Then you come up with these theories, i.e., matter is composed of small particles, molecules, etc. Who has seen a molecule? Nobody has seen a molecule, but you studied how these things work when there are chemical changes made; how they work when a physical change is made; and you study them with your five senses, not with imagination; not with the Holy Ghost. It doesn't work in this field.

G_d pointed Muhammed to five senses

Here is Muhammed is being talked to by G_d Almighty and He is pointing not to his sixth sense. G_d pointed to Muhammed's five senses. That is what you need to educate yourself and produce your society. Mr. Fard said, "Think five times before you speak and maybe you'll be correct". First, use your five senses before anything else. "He taught man what he was not knowing before" (Qur'an). Isn't that a fact? Allah is bringing Muhammed to see that if man has science and knowledge it is because G_d provided him with the tool of his own creation with the creation to support and give its benefits to that tool; man as a tool. And that is how you became educated. Before you were knowing anything you were helpless without G_d's support from His creation; without G_d designing you in the way that you are designed. So this is endearing Muhammed to his Lord and enriching him with knowledge and understanding so he can become the leader for the whole of humanity, for all people.

"Isn't man a very ungrateful creature?"

Then G_d points out something saying, "You see, Muhammed, what I showed you in these few verses? Now, isn't man a very ungrateful creature? He has been withholding all of this from you. He used My creation to develop his life and his world, to build and get things in his own name and glory. Isn't he very ungrateful in that he is not acknowledging his Lord, the Creator Who made all this possible for him?"

So when Muhammed saw that he understood what his mission was and what he was going to do one day; that he had to become a new educator, not discussing things and hiding G_d, the One Who made it possible; but discussing things and acknowledging G_d. So he was given a mission to be a witness that G_d is One, G_d exists and G_d is our Benefactor. G_d is the One Who made everything that we benefit from and he got a great following.

Human body is the sign of G_d

The human body itself is a structure of great knowledge and science, if you accept that the human body is the ayat (sign) of G_d. G_d says there are ayats, signs, in the heavens and in the earth as well as within yourself; G_d's ayats. The Arabic word, ayat, means verses, statements, readings in the Qur'an. But in this focus where G_d says, "In the sky are ayats and in the earth are ayats, as well as in yourselves," this is not a direct reading. This is a reading by way of interpretation or by the way of translation. You have to translate the objects in the heavens and be inspired by G_d to know how to connect the language of the heavens with your own intelligence; so that you read the script that G_d wrote when He wrote, when He created the sky up there, when He threw the skies out into existence; and then the earth the same. You have to be able to translate, to see, what is G_d saying with a rain drop. This is philosophical. But this is how education began.

The creation uses the scientist as a tool to express itself

The philosopher, the thinker, was before the exact sciences, or the true sciences. I don't know why we call them the true sciences. These are not true sciences. These are true tools of creation and that is all he (the scientist) is. He is a tool of creation. He thinks he is using creation and it is using him to express itself and give itself to more people. He is nothing but a tool of creation. And the proof of it is the creation says, "Don't use your brain, just watch me. Just keep digging into me and studying me. Just look at what I have inside of me and share it with others".

2

How to Live in Community

So we are told by divine guidance, the revelation from the inspired to the communities of the heavenly religions of father Abraham, that we go through stages; one dark environment to a second one; then from that second one to a third one and then deliverance; three stages of darkness or light, perception, breaking through three veils of darkness: home, public, education, to find what? How to live in community.

How to Live in Community

G_d made the human soul to live in peace, to live in clean space and to have order, not a bunch of confusion all around it. So the child won't know why it is behaving badly or wanting to be violent and you will not know. You will say, "I'm going to have that boy to see a psychiatrist." Before you do that let the psychiatrist come and see the space the boy lives in and you might save yourself some money.

Space is very important. We are talking about life and how it starts. A little smaller germ that we can't see with our physical eyes becomes a full human person in the environment we call the body of mama. And then it is delivered out into our world and somebody gives us a lot of help. But it seems that we can't get to benefit from the help anymore.

Mother Earth, another mother

You were living on the body of mama, getting all your needs from her body. Now you are out here with the family and you are living on Mother Earth and she is supporting your life just as your mother's body supported your life when you were confined in her. Now something should come to your mind if you make these connections. Here I am in my mama existing as nothing. Nobody could see it with their physical eye. But there formed a complete human being in that confinement, in that dark place. Then, I'm delivered out into the world and they tell me I'm living now on Mother Earth and I need her, too, for all my life needs such as food, clothing, shelter, and transportation, whatever. And it seems I have light out here. The sun is shining.

Another dark place

I have light. But for most of us, we are in a dark place, just as we were when we were in our mothers. We are in another dark place. The light is on but you cannot see how to direct yourself. But if you would just rest like that baby did in its mother and accept help from all the directions that are coming, you would do something with your life out here in what you call daylight or sunlight. Your life would be helped because the good people, they will give you what you need. The good teachers they will love your peace, not your piece that shoots and kills; your p-e-a-c-e.; your quiet, your peace of mind; your faith in the new environment; that it can support me like the one that supported me when I was a germ and could not make myself; i.e., Mother Earth.

When you go back and look at your beginning in your mother and you come under her supervision and she turns you over to the public and to the world, that was one darkness; then, you come into the world, into another darkness; and then you go to school, you to go to college, you get degrees and you think you see. But, it is another darkness.

How to live in community

So we are told by divine guidance, the revelation from the inspired to the communities of the heavenly religions of father Abraham, that we go through stages; one dark environment to a second one; then from that second one to a third one and then deliverance; three stages of darkness or light, perception, breaking through three veils of darkness: home, public, education, to find what? How to live in community. You can go to college and get all of your degrees and come out and you still do not know how to live in community. Many of us with those degrees can't even make a decent home life for ourselves. We can't be faithful to one wife. We can't keep important matters in order according to their priorities.

So we fail at home, fail on the job. The Ph. D gets fired and we find him drunk. He can't stand up to it. He cannot understand it. He has a lot of questions that he does not have answers for. He wants somebody to explain things to him, but he has a Ph. D. So he goes to see a psychiatrist and sometimes a psychiatrist is psyched out before he gets there. But if you do not have your heart right, if you don't have your mind right, if you don't have your spirit right, if you are not in a disposition to respect things that are due respect, it is all darkness. You cannot see. We have to change that.

Take your life to a place of safety

We need space. When G_d tells us of man being put in the Garden and that garden was a safe and pleasant space for him, G_d is not telling us of what happened in our past. G_d is giving us a projection. G_d is telling us where He wants us to take our life. Take your life to a place of safety, to a place of cleanliness, to a place of love, to a place of concern for one another. And don't let the deceiver convert you to rationalize on your own and make an independent decision for your life where you take it without respecting priorities. G_d says this world is bigger than you, and if you don't have His guidance you cannot manage it. It is going to, eventually, drive you crazy or bring you down to destruction.

G_d Created All Human Beings as One People

In the Qur'an Allah (G_d), Most High, says, "You are the best community evolved for mankind, Kuntum khaira ummatin ukhrijat lin naas." The word is "Kuntum" and it means, "You were". But the scholars understand that it means, "You are"; like when it says in the Qur'an, "Kaanan naasu ummatan wahidah, the people were once one united community", in the beginning of time. But that same expression, the scholars understand it to mean that mankind, presently, should be seen as one family of human beings, or one community of human beings and isn't that true?

Ants, they live with ants and whether they live in Atlanta, or Chicago, they live the same way and they all are a community of ants. There is a chapter called, *Ants*, in the Qur'an and it doesn't say the ants of the North. It just says ants. Ants are ants, although they have differences. You put mice with ants and you know that is a different family, different life; the same thing for the mosquitoes or anything else. Human beings, you find them all alike all over. Wherever you find them in any part of the world they look alike and they can become alike. Even if they speak different languages they can learn to speak with each other in the same language. They may dress differently, but they can change their dress and dress alike. They can be different in whatever way but they all can change and be just alike if they want to. If they come and adopt, come into the other's environment and adopt the ways of the other they become just alike; no different.

People began life on this earth as one community

I used to see white folks dancing on television a long time ago and they used to dance like they had stilts in their pants and springs on the bottom of the stilts. Now, when they dance I can't tell the difference in the African American and them. They dance just alike. They sing alike. They play music alike. They've blended right in. Do you see? So we are one human family and G_d said that to the people. He gave that in the Bible and He said that with the Qur'an. He said that to the Muslims, that we are one people, one family, "Kaanan naasu ummtan wahidah, the people were one community".

If you understand the language of Arabic how the logic goes, when Allah says that, it is like somebody telling you a story; and they say, "Time was standing still." But you know time is moving. So you know when they tell you that they are coming forward, can't go backwards. They have to come forward because you know time doesn't stand still. So when G_d says the people were once one community, what comes into your mind is that before that time there were no people. "Kaanan naasu ummatin waahidah, the people were one community". Before that time that G_d is addressing there were no people. He is saying that people began as one community. That is exactly what it means, that people began their life on this earth as one community. Does it mean they were all in Arabia or all in Africa, Japan, or somewhere? No, it means that they were all like the ants that I mentioned earlier. No matter where they were they walked like ants. They hunted food like ants. They made communities like ants. That is what He means; not that they were all in one place.

Boundaries of Authority

It happens that very often I say to myself, "Where is the authority in our life?" Authority is environment-based. In much of the world today there is human suffering. The growing world is requiring that more of us grow. Religion, school, parents, government, fell down from their once strong authority in our lives, in the life of parents, and the youth. Many good parents tell us it's extremely difficult to plan life for their youth in a culture of violence and drugs.

How to Live in Community

In our natural make-up is the created nature and spirit to want to compete. In a wild jungle environment competition is ruthless. In a human society competition is expected to be civilized. Desire for progress is the influence serving the advancement of society. It can lose its good condition and influence progress to grow out of human control. The drug culture is not human. The culture of violence is not human. Our learning environment may be working to intimidate our better human impulses and force our better human impulses into a retreat and out of conscience.

Identifying environmental boundary lines

Our plan to save our youth is an effort to simplify the way we want our youth to look at authority. "Authority", according to *Funk and Wagnalls Standard Dictionary*, is, "The right to command and enforce obedience." Authority is seen in association with that in which the right of authority originates something, requires obedience, protection, care, etc. We see authority in association with environmental boundaries. The boundary holding within it all other boundaries is thought to be the universe. When that obedience to that within that boundary is identified we find that there are many smaller boundaries of obedience.

The authority associated with environmental boundaries may be scaled inwardly from that most distant boundary line-the boundary of the universe. Thus, in identifying environmental boundary lines there is the boundary of all space considered as a whole, the environment of the sun and earth; the earth with its boundary line of living space, legal boundaries of independent nations with their governments; the smaller boundary lines within national boundaries; and, lastly, the boundary line of private space; that is, private, human space, or human dwelling space. Whatever exists requiring obedience, protection, care control, etc., is a basis for establishing authority.

Boundary of representative authority

Boundaries may serve as reference for measuring and ordering authority along lines of urgency and priority. The authority over the obedience of the bodies that are in the community of the stars would have no way of not destroying those bodies of stars if those bodies rejected that obedience. The profound, philosophical, inescapable truth is all authority is in the sphere and boundary of representative authority. To some extent, our big problem of cruelty to self and others is a protest of our first nature, protesting against arbitrary authority's pressuring us to establish representative authority.

The Nation of Islam in America was conceived by the foreigner, Fard (spelled F-a-r-d). Fard, the extremely radical and unorthodox sort of mystic, boldly gave the plan he formed the label, "Islam", the Nation of Islam, and the Holy Temples of Islam. When he was questioned by the FBI Fard claimed authority and authorization upon the authority of the sacred book of the faithful Muslims of the world, Middle Eastern Muslims, African Muslims, Asian Muslims, European Muslims, all identifying the supreme authority in their life to be the word of G_d, the Koran, properly called the Qur'an.

The foreigner, Fard, who dressed himself in mystery, created for us a controlled environment. A young African student, seeking a doctorate degree, for his dissertation interviewed many members of the Nation of Islam, both top leaders and the members in the general congregation. Among those he interviewed was Mr. Elijah Mohammed, himself. E. Assien Udom identified an attempt to provide black Americans a cultural identity as the purpose in the creation of Fard's Nation of Islam in America. Udom's book was titled, *Black Nationalism*. It came on the market some years ahead of Dr. C. Eric Lincoln's book and classical work, *The Black Muslims in America*. This information, recalled, provides some background.

A language environment of our own was more an influence serving to hold the members of the Nation to a life-plan than was the influence and power of the FOI (Fruit of Islam), with its militant captains and Nation of Islam law enforcement. That experience influenced us to keep an interest in a language environment of our own. Today, we have a language environment of our own bearing the new, strong imprint of our present, spiritual, social and philosophical thinking and orientation. Owing much to the interest in a language environment of our own, we are today realizing more success for our private school system and we think for all of our productive affairs.

How to Live in Community

Conscious youth should be given more importance

Popular cultural society is selling our youth bigger-than-real life expectations. Our youth believe that they are entitled to have whatever they see as the present lifestyle or popular lifestyle, today. Our plan to save our youth is against a treatment of our youth that gives popularity and importance to reckless youth. Our treatment should not say the reckless youth is more in need of recognition from us. The conscious youth should be more in the news and be accorded more importance in our eyes. We believe ratings would go up for the media that would accept this way of helping the reckless youth and the conscious youth to know their value. The value of the two should not be confused. A drug pusher should be in convict clothes whenever on television. If that were done the network ratings would go up.

Can sexual appetite be exaggerated to the point that sexual appetite threatens to take control from society, from individuals, from parents? There is a blues song. It goes, "I believe myself you are the devil in nylon hose. The harder I work, the faster my money goes". And Big Joe Turner sang another old goodie. It goes like this, "Now flip, flop and fly. I don't care if I die. Just don't ever leave me. Don't ever say, 'good-bye'." It is such influence and many other negative influences that invade the most inward parts of our life. They come in with such innocence. It is such influence that makes it all the more urgent that we be responsible for our own language environment; a language environment that has as its most important concern the influence of correct education.

With no awareness of harm done many parents make their children feel that lifeless objects bought with money and their material image of success are more important matters than children themselves. When parents say to the child, "Get off of my sofa, stay out of my refrigerator, don't touch my things, I own this house", we're putting distances between us and our children and we are making them feel small, making them feel that they don't possess anything. And I believe that this language, if it's not used, our language environment will be much more conducive to decency and industry in our children. We should want that we never say anything or treat our children in any way that would contribute to the already existing problem of thinking we are not well-situated, humanly.

Thoughts for Searchers

Superior identity, the same in everybody

The human heritage is human decency and intelligence. This heritage is the first heritage and the more enduring heritage. Islam says to us superior identify is the same in everybody. The picture the Creator shows us challenges us from within. That picture is the picture of our first heritage, or our first inheritance. It is the picture of our evolving human design, its growing capacity and potential. The pride that this identity supports promises us much more than a race pride that is concentrated mostly in our awareness of the difference of our skin color or features, or the texture of our hair.

Our flesh body was created to be our helper. I remember my loving and strong mother obligating me to be responsible for getting out of bed early enough to be successful each day. I had to boss myself. I would say, "Wallace, lying here in bed feels so good, but get up right now! Go to the washroom! Finish what you have to do there and return to the bedroom and dress! Leave your area in good order and be on the way to arrive at school on time!" When it was not school, it was chores in or outside, or a job from which I earned an income.

Early in my life I became aware of my flesh body as my faithful helper and friend. It was pleasant and intriguing to remember how sleepy I was at times and how difficult for me it was to brush my teeth before going to bed. I remember my body's fatigue; how I had gone to sleep; how my body remembered to hold on to what was in its hand and how my body awoke on time without me standing over it. Our flesh body can be observed in its role of friend and helper.

Life is the same everywhere

On our interest in having our own word or language environment, what it means to us in our program of education for our youth and their future, our plan is to strengthen education in the life of our youth. We want to show the working relationship for the flesh package and the person contained inside the package. Observation, revelation, and science show the flesh body existing as the medium and means through which and by which the person inside is to have expression. This life is the same everywhere on earth for every human being.

How to Live in Community

We don't sneeze in Russian or in English. We don't laugh or cry differently. We don't yawn and cough in a certain language. The presence of a citizen of black skin and woolly hair on the same elevator with a citizen of white skin does not darken the elevator for the white citizen who is not trying to disown the common first-life relationship. Our first life neither knows nor accepts racism.

A few years ago, Carole Mosley Braun, the former senator from Illinois, said to an audience, "The future will require that we shift public attention from race to diversity". In this awareness of unity and diversity is a support for genuine freedom. Our plan to save our youth is a plan to have our youth know the whole of their functioning existence.

Spiraling boundaries

As a further note on the context for those existing boundary lines mentioned earlier, an increased awareness of those extending boundaries for our existence serves the life of our created industrious spirit. Created obedience is signaled all the way from the most distant regions of this universe into our most private quarters, into our life inside our flesh bodies. Precious life support may be missing in us because our life is out of touch with the soul's need to be in touch with the spiraling boundaries out of which the human self emerges.

The native space of our mind

The key to inner peace waits for the achievement of peaceful boundaries or peaceful borders in conscience, since the distance to which the human mind can travel and dwell is as a country land for one's mind. There should be peace for the mind on all borders in the vast sphere of the human mind. The better education serves to bridge the gaps which may cut off the life flow, the freedom, and the peace, that come into the soul with a recognition of our extended existence over the boundaries of our native space, the native space of our mind. Family, town, nation, and the international community are all circles for the existence of our life and borders that we must establish peace with for the healthy and productive conditions of our souls.

When the way life that is lived does not make sense, most likely it's that the first nature and the person have stopped talking to each other. Persons seriously preparing themselves to be responsible for the human structuring of their lives will not be far away from proving themselves responsible for the material structures in their community.

Pampering us hurts our created nobility

At one time in our economic history big business monopolies have threatened to weaken democracy and its free enterprise system. I remember how African American neighborhoods in Chicago were before the coming of urban renewal. Some conditions were helped. I never wished for the return of the city's conditions that were before urban renewal. However, there was a brighter business future in sight before the coming of the community-connecting expressways and fast food chains. There was established over our neighborhoods a stealthy monopoly which turned the lights out on our hope of growing to one day supply our quarters with needed businesses: industries, financial institutions, and whatever is to be desired in us for growth in intelligence, ingenuity, and in the total resources of a free people.

On behalf of the future generations, on behalf of the future of our youth, we want America to know we don't want our government to use taxes to pay for social programs that put pampers on our men. Pampering us hurts our created nobility and dignity. We wish our nation and private enterprise to regard all citizens as equal members in the American family of citizens. We wish that we not be blocked from achieving progress, social development and self-supported stable communities.

We have a prayer that we say, privately, or with others. That prayer is, "Our Lord, give us from among ourselves mates (wives) to delight our eyes and make from us a leader for the conscious people." (Qur'an)

Need for strong moral leadership

The problem in our society that bothers us perhaps more than any other problem is the support that is given to leaders who obviously don't care if their audience is conscious or not, who play on a tendency in their audience to be subjected to blind impulses. We are not getting the kind of leaders that we were getting at the end of slavery; leaders like Frederick Douglass and the many men and women in that tradition. We are not looking to support leaders who have strong moral principles and strong faith in the excellent created nature in man.

We hope that our youth will turn away from leaders who fish in the waters of our weaknesses. We hope that from our future generations we will have principles and be true to the noble purpose and serve our best interest and noble aspirations. This is our hope. We don't believe that any real change is going to come until we address the need to have a better condition within ourselves.

When our hearts bother us and our intelligence regards what is in our best interest, we will see change for the better and responsible communities serving our needs and contributing to the beauty and strength of America. We accept the plural nature of our society and we welcome the challenge to be more responsible, more productive, and less dependent on help from the government or from other groups in this plural society of America.

Way to better citizenship

We hope that our youth will get strength from our language and identify with the Muslim spirit, with their community, and with their nation, the United States of America. We believe that citizens who claim citizenship, freedom, and responsibility for themselves and a share in the responsibility of their nation and its future security and prosperity will be situated to have a better existence and a brighter future. This is what we want to put in the language environment of the community for ourselves, but more importantly, to save our youth from destroying themselves.

3

All Life Out of Water

Water is symbolic of many things of the human being but mostly the sentiments of the human being. We cry tears. That is water. We cry tears of joy, pleasure, and sadness. Those produce tears for us. That is the water. It is where they originally get the water. These are heavenly waters that come down from the eyes. Then you have lower waters, the waters of the psyche. And they speak of sweet tears and salty tears.

All Life Out of Water

When Muhammed said, "Make good use of five before five be your failing or cause you to be defeated, to lose", he meant make good use of five senses. The sense to smell, to taste, to feel, to see, the sense to hear, make good use of these five senses before five become your downfall. What are the five that will be your downfall? The same five, neglected, will be your downfall. The Qur'an says, "Whoever spends on his own soul succeeds and whoever neglects it fails." How do we spend on our own soul? Spend on your five senses and you will be spending on your own soul. You will refine your soul. You will enrich your soul. You will elevate your soul, if you try. Strive to make the best use of your five senses.

We have the sense of taste, but human life wants to taste only that which is suitable for human life. There are animals that like to eat filth. Their nature is to clean up the filth on earth. We have taste but we don't want their taste. So a human being with human intelligence wants to always refine his taste, elevate his taste, make better his taste and he wants to be more selective so he will be identified as a creature having better, higher and more decent choices for taste. Look at the pride we enjoy when we are intelligent and refined in the culture. Look at the pride that we sense when we sit down at the table and eat very nice tasting food and we are bringing it to each other's attention asking, "How do you like that? What does that taste like? It is terrific. It is very tasty." All creatures don't have that.

Progressing senses

All of our senses are progressing senses. They are not senses that are at a standstill. They are growing senses. They are senses that are reaching for higher and higher consciousness. That is true for the sight, hearing, all of them. We don't hear to hear the noise or sound or to know how loud something was. We hear to know how worthy of my ear or how worthy our ear something is; and we say, "That is foolishness. I don't have any time to try to hear that. That's vulgar. My eyes don't want to look at that." Look how wonderful our senses are. If we take the pains or take the time to elevate our senses then we enrich our soul, we structure our souls better and we succeed in life. If we do the reverse we neglect our own souls and we bring our life down to the lowest of the low. This is

Qur'an, the teachings of Al Islam. And it is so clear when you stay on tract. But when you are out there skipping and jumping all about the universe for understanding you miss all of this. So come home to the standing place of Abraham. Begin there and stay focused and you won't be lost in the twilight zone, or to the twilight zone. Praise be to Allah.

Higher life for all people

Al Islam is the fulfillment of what is told in Jesus Christ as a mystery. The birth of Jesus Christ is a mystery and in the nativity there are animals, not just a man, not just human life. There are other forms of life. Why? Because the five senses are in animals just like they are in us. And that is to say that whatever G_d is going to do with this model man, Jesus Christ, the life that he is going to be working with is also in animals; the life of intelligence, the life of the five senses. But He has created this man to become the supreme model of life higher than all the animals for all people of the world. Jesus Christ is a sign of that.

Jesus' mystery to protect truth

Then Muhammed, the Prophet, comes and he is a man living in history, a historical testimony to what Allah tells us in a mysterious picture of the nativity. I'm convinced that when Muhammed, the Prophet, said, "They will see me and Christ Jesus together," he was talking about more than just the Prophets as brothers or the family of Prophets, that they all belong to one family in mankind. I know he was talking about more than that. He was talking about what is very important in scripture or in revelation and what is important is the mystery of Jesus Christ. Why is he a mystery? He is a mystery because man had not evolved enough in his time in the sciences, in the study of G_d's creation, in the study of nature that G_d made. He hadn't evolved enough in that to really have language references to support him receiving that knowledge and his world was so savage and barbaric at the time that if it was told they would make every attempt to destroy it before it got to people.

So it was done also to protect the truth for a time when the environment or the circumstances for it surviving and not being persecuted so severely would be there waiting for a better time. It was hidden for a better time, for the intelligence of the people but also for the safety in the environment or a safe situation for it in the environment when the rulers would not be so barbaric and savage and ignorant themselves. So it worked.

There is so much in revelation that I could give you to support this. That is what I look for you to do. When you read you will see all this support that I'm giving. As you read scripture you will see the support just coming, plenty of it supporting what I'm saying. So there is no need of me going through all of that with you. You will see it, you will read it. You will find it and you will give it, some of you, like you discovered it for the first time; and you won't even remember me giving it to you. That is okay, too. It is okay with me. I'll be happy. Just benefit from it and share it.

In my conclusion on that which I have been commenting on I say to you that there is not a nation that we know on this earth that does not have a star in its flag. Am I right or wrong? I don't know of one. Someone may say, "I don't think there is a star in the Japanese flag?" Well what does science say the sun is? It is the closest star feeding our life, the sun. It is a star. But don't think the Japanese don't have it. They have stars, too; maybe not in the flag there, but they have other symbols and governmental emblems and things. They have the star also. Every star you know of except the star in the Jewish flag or the Jewish sacred symbol has five points. Don't they? For the Jew is it six. But for most of the people it is a five point star.

Common sense established by using the five senses

So the majority of the world has acknowledged five points. I don't care if you call it five points. Don't call it star but just realize that all nations, the great majority of them, even Israel, recognize five too, but they don't have it. They have the Star of David with six points. They have five points. When this country protested against the treatment of the British crown or the British government and decided to have a revolution against British authority and dominance in their life, one of the great patriots who came to awaken the minds of the thirteen colonies, the public over here in the new world to resist being dominated by Britain, he (Thomas Paine) came up with a paper called, *Common Sense*.

We find that the recognition of relationships and the bonding for human beings in the history of the founding of this great society are the five senses and he caused them to come together upon recognition that all of us have this life. We have five senses and we have common sense because we make big use of our five senses and we can be established upon common sense. Our argument is based upon common sense.

We are all creatures of five senses

Don't bring the Bible into this. Don't bring the theories of the old world into this. Let us unite on the strength that we all are creatures of five senses and this is our common excellence, our common life. And what does not jell well or does not make sense to our five senses let us reject it even though papa Britain says we have to listen to it. This was the argument, mankind uniting upon the power of the five senses and identifying their life as one common life; and if they practice the best of their five senses they will have common sense strong enough to support their cause and their rebellion against the authority of Britain in their lives over here in the new world, in the colonies.

More importance on your intelligence

So you should put more importance on your intelligence. Muhammed said Allah never created anything more productive than the human brain. Look in your world and tell me what did all this? What built this building? What designed these things? What brought electricity to us? What do we owe all of this to? How did all of this get started? It got started when someone began using his brain or her brain. All of this is the result of somebody using the brain. We didn't have anything but just the dirt, ground, the trees, the natural world, until somebody started using the brain. Then, we became great producers, creators ourselves, because of the brain.

Never disrespect your creation as an intelligent person in this creation, in this world of matter or material things. You're intelligent. You are created to be intelligent. You are a creator. You are a great producer. You can become so productive that you relieve miseries in other nations and on the earth where people are suffering. You can become so productive because of this brain.

All Life Out of Water

Never see yourself with animals. See yourself distinguished because of your brain.

A promise of life

In the New Testament it is said that Jesus Christ fed the multitude with two fish and five loaves of bread. There is five again. The word "multitude" gives to our mind's the picture of a lot of people. This was not a regular gathering of people. This was a great gathering of people. It is really a future picture. It is not talking about the one back then. It is giving to the mind that he had gathered a great number of people around him back at that time, but it is a projection. It is talking about the future, that there will be people from different nations, multitudes of people and they will be fed by five loaves of bread.

How do you make bread?

Prophet Abraham in his true picture as an intelligent human being called, "Haneef", stood upon two feet or two fish and five senses, five loaves of bread. What is bread? How do you make bread? You take what looks like dust, called flour. It looks like dust and you begin preparing it, add water to suit it to your taste, milk, or whatever. You put something in it that breathes into the bread, called yeast. You put yeast into it and the yeast breathes into the bread. The breath of the yeast causes the bread to swell. It becomes lighter. It won't be flat bread. It will be dinner rolls, loaves of bread. You put it in the heat after you cause it to rise and the heat cooks it. The heat makes it rise more. Heat expands things. It rises and becomes a beautiful loaf of bread.

Heat symbolic of love or extreme passion

The smooth layer on the top looks like the skin of a newborn baby. Then you say we have bread. You eat the bread. The bread comes from a seed of a plant life called wheat and the wheat grass grows very tall. It stands up very straight. It stands upright, straight. This is all symbolic, metaphorical. That is what the language is. Why do you need heat? Heat can be love, but heat can also be passions that have gone to the extreme. When you submit the life that exists now only in a promise you can hardly see it. It is like a seed. A seed is a promise that you are going to have wheat grass, or you are going to have a corn stalk with ears of corn. So it is for human life that G_d creates before it evolves or blossoms into what Allah wants to bring out of it. It is like a promise. And the promise is small, unattractive. It is not exciting like to seed of something that is going to become a beautiful picture. But in its seed it is not attractive, it does not excite anybody.

Bread symbolic of your intelligence potential

The human seed, if you subject it to passions of love and fire, those passions heat up, makes them very hot. Whether they become passions destructive or not that fire that is cooking this bread, if you put it on you it is going to kill you. It will burn you up. Put you in the oven with the bread and you will die. Put some life you have in the oven with the bread and it is going to kill it, destroy it. But the bread survives it, because the bread is symbolic of your intelligence and your intelligent potential, those five senses; five loaves of bread.

Subject it to extreme heat, to an environment of extreme passions where it is unbearable for life to exist there, you may die, your whole generation may die. But eventually, the essence, the intelligence will survive in others and just their experiencing the burning furnace or the burning oven is going to inspire in them new hopes in the intelligence, a new straining on the part of the human intelligence to overcome these difficulties and do things.

Wheat grass as human urges

When we look back at the history of how the five senses survive and how they bring intelligence in new opportunities for us; when we look back at it, it began as something that started with an unattractive thing like a grain of wheat, a seed of grass, But it stood its life up straight and it attracted mankind to want to taste it and want to eat it and want to feed his own life with it. Now, we are not talking about the wheat grass as wheat grass. We are talking about wheat grass as human urges in our intelligence that wants to stand us up straight. Then we're going to feed on righteousness on uprightness. And as a people in the history of the world we're going to struggle much. We are going to come through much heat. We are going to even have animal essence in our bread. But the animal essence is going to be influenced by the heat and come under the effect or influence of the heat; and in the environment of our bread, the uprightness even of the animal is going to contribute to enlarging the mass.

"Let us break bread"

It's going to become bigger but lighter and more chewable, not so tough to chew with your mental teeth. All of this is talking about human intelligence, the mind. Then you are going to look back on it. One day you are going to look back on that history of how you came from a little unattractive life just wanting to be upright and how that life under the influences of society, the strain and torment it had to experience, it turned out to be a beautiful loaf of bread. Here is man reviewing the history of his rise from an unattractive life, but wanting to be upright, to a civilized, blooming society, blossoming and blooming world. And he sees it as something coming from a wheat grain and now it's a beautiful loaf of bread.

When they sit down and say, "Let us break bread," they have much more on their mind if they know what they are doing than what we think when we see somebody saying, "Let us break bread." Those who break bread with this knowledge, they are qualified to protect civilization for the future.

Moral thinking and moral life in the water of intelligence

So what are the two fish? The two fish are the ability of your mind to see left and right; to see ahead and behind; to see down and up; to see truth and falsehood; to see decency and indecency. Isn't that how the moral mind works? So the two fish are moral thinking and moral life in the water. The two fish represent the moral life in the water of intelligence, or in the soul that has intelligence, to look and make distinctions; to distinguish between truth and falsehood; to distinguish between darkness and light; to distinguish between indecency and what is decent. This is an important, fundamental life activity in the human intelligence. The Qur'an says He began all life in water. The man had been formed in the earth but he couldn't progress until G_d caused it to rain upon the earth and then he fashioned the man. He was already there but he had not been fashioned. Then Allah causes the heavens to rain and wet the dry ground; and then He formed him and breathed into him of His spirit or His will and he became a living soul.

Sweet and salty waters

Water is symbolic of human sensitivities; the same thing for psyche. Water is symbolic of many things of the human being, but mostly the sentiments of the human being. We cry tears. That is water. We cry tears of joy, pleasure and sadness. Those produce tears for us. That is the water. These are heavenly waters that come down from the eyes. Then you have lower waters, the waters of the psyche. And they speak of sweet tears and salty tears.

They also speak of sweet waters and salty waters. Salty water is the ocean and the lakes and rivers are sweet water. All of this is referring right back to human beings. This language stems from the study of human nature and the building of the human sciences. That is where all this language comes from. We can read about rivers, lakes, in geography. That is not the same as reading about rivers, lakes, and oceans in the Qur'an, or in scripture.

A three day journey

I was doing dikhr (reflecting on G_d by reciting His names or attributes) and I noticed that the lines go straight up for the two lower parts of my fingers...the lines go straight. The first one goes straight up. The second one goes straight. The third one goes in a circle. That's the universe. So in Islamic dhikr it is showing us, if you just start at the base, in the nature, and if you can just stay straight after the nature, G_d will eventually put you in the universe...You can be reborn and free.

In the Bible, it's free (you will be freed). It says, "And on the 5th day G_d created the creatures that fly freely in the heavens"; the birds. According to Islam it's on the 3rd day. We say the 3rd progression; only two progressions take you into the heavens. They call it two progressions. The third situation is heaven. It's in the Bible, too. That was with Jonah when he said, "I have a three day journey". His being released by the big fish is symbolic of being born out of the womb of your mother, being delivered from your mother. And that isn't the end of it. That's the end of that particular situation, but there's another situation to follow.

So it starts with our birth. Everything starts with the human being and the human body as a sign. But it doesn't stop there. It goes from there to the signs that are in G_d's universe, the earth and the heavens. If I were to say to somebody, "The big fish is the womb of your mother and the delivery of Jonah from the big fish is the same as the delivery or your birth from your mother, they might say, "Ah, he doesn't know that!" Why don't I know? Is it because I didn't say the rest of it? Why should I anyway? If I want to make that point, that's the point that I'm making.

The big fish is the religious order

The big fish is the religious order. The Church or the spiritual world is the big fish. And the big fish swallows you up. But if you are rational you can't be peaceful in the big fish. Once you get rational the big fish has no more taste for you. The big fish spits you out on land. "No, you don't belong in the water!" And that's what happened to Jonah, but both in himself and in the spiritual world. It has reference to both, not just one. And when he was spat out, he was spat out on a desert (seashore). The seashore is very seldom furnished with greenery. If it is, it's high up. It will be high up if there is any greenery. The water is low, running very low. But if it is on the same level the water will come up there and wash everything away and kill everything near the sea or the water.

So he was thrown out on something like that and then the gourd plant tells you that there is not much growing there. It is like a barren land. The Qur'an says a little gourd plant grew over him as a mercy from G_d and covered his head from the sunlight; gave him some shade. And in that situation he said, "I have a three day journey". The gourd plant, it represents scarcity of food. The gourd doesn't give you much but a lot of seeds. It doesn't give you much. The gourd plant is like squash, pumpkin. It gives you a lot, but not much. It gives you a lot of seeds but not much meat that you like. You would take the seed part out and throw that out and eat the outer part, the rind, the hull and it isn't much. There's not much to like. So, that was his (Jonah's) first situation.

Thoughts for Searchers

Figment of your imagination

Now you know the gourd plant is big and it's given in the Bible, again, when it mentions the fig tree. Jesus came to the fig tree and the Bible, the Gospel, says he cursed it because it didn't have any fruit on it. So since it didn't have any fruit on it he cursed it not to bear fruit anymore. And I used to look at that and I'd say, "That's cruel, man. That pure, innocent tree, why would he want to hurt the tree?" Well, when I came to understand it, it is very beautiful.

There's an English expression, "That's a figment of your imagination." So, the knowledge is still in the world. Evidence of it is this expression in the West, "That's a figment of your imagination". And, "It's a figment". It's spelled "f-i-g", fig, and it's "ment". It's a figment of your imagination. And if you look at fig you can see where the word "figure" came from, too; nothing but figures; no problem solved, just figures.

Now, the condition that you need to have life is water. If there's no water life cannot have a beginning. That's what it means, that your beginning is in water. Now, we're not talking about the physical body, but it's true for the physical body, too. That's why they're saying that science and religion are coming together. It's true for the physical body, but it's not talking about the physical body. It's talking about the mind.

You know, the thinking process that brings you, eventually, to understand this universe, that's what it's talking about. And the beginning of that thinking process has to be in your sentiments. It doesn't form in your rational mind, first. It forms in your sentiments, in your feelings. You have to be concerned for life and the future of life and thinking starts there. That's the beginning of that thinking, in the water.

Inherent perception

In the picture of Jesus Christ in the New Testament the woman is crying and using her tears, her water, to clean his feet, his foundation, what he stands upon. Actually, she uses her hair, her inherent perception, strong perception. A gnat can touch your hair and you know it, because it's as though the hair's roots go beneath the surface of the skin; and the communication or vibration goes directly to the nerve center.

So hair is always a mystery and symbolic of the spiritual sense, the inner sense, or inherent sense and it's in all animals. A rooster, when he is afraid for his life in a fight his feathers come up. A bull or a dog when he's in danger his hair comes up. So, noticing this over a long period of time, man got the idea that this is the inner sense and it's more powerful than seeing, feeling with the hands.

Phases of moon symbolic of thinking process trying to find reality

On the Hajj (Pilgrimage), when we complete the rites, we cut the hair. Its benefits are not enough to depend on. It becomes instinct, something that stinks on the inside. When the real thing comes, that's stinking inside. So when you finish sa'iy (the Hajj ritual of running between two hills) then you go cut your hair. And that's all instinct, because all that inner sense can do is to go between one extreme and the other (running between the two hills). It can never be free. It has to run between one extreme and another like the moon. It starts with the crescent moon and it goes through phases till it's black and then it starts all over, again. And that just keeps going on forever. It can never complete itself. Every time it completes itself it has to die; die to what it thought was straight. And that's all the moon is symbolic of, your thinking process trying to find reality. Your thinking process, it goes from, in appearance, oppression and it is trying to complete itself. And every time it completes itself it's not satisfied. It's not satisfied with its conclusion. So then it starts throwing off what it has gathered until it gets back to nothing, again. It just keeps repeating that, like Sisyphus trying to get that big round rock up on the side of the hill. Every time he lets it go it starts rolling back down the hill.

Man's life as worker under G_d never finished

So really, it's a process that takes us from innocent nature, straining. You're straining. It's the path of uprightness and you are straining your nature. If you are straining your conscious you can preserve the innocence of your nature and become that life in conscious; and you're still striving for reality, striving for the whole truth. Eventually, G_d is going to reveal to you and you're going to come into the freedom of the universe. G_d says in the Qur'an, "And when you are free from you immediate task still labor hard". Man's life as far as a worker under G_d is never finished. There is too much left for us to be idle or retired. So as soon as we complete something, no matter how important it was, we should right away devote ourselves to another task.

We Are All Orphans

We are all orphans and we have to be connected back with our true parent. The true parent is the natural person who feels his/her existence on this earth is an existence with the material world itself; an existence with the land that produces food, clothing, shelter; an existence with that land. Manhood needs man to know himself as a product of the earth, evolved or born out of the earth to work the earth and use it for himself and for the benefit of others. Your manhood needs that. If you will accept that then that is your purpose. That is why you are existing. You will become a better person for yourself, a better person for others, especially your family and you will become productive.

There is no such thing as one race being inferior to another, one race can produce and another one cannot, one race is protecting its race and another race is not protecting its race. So whether you are Spanish, African American, or whatever, you are, if your race is doing badly, poorly, dependent on other nationalities, other races, other communities, or other ethnic groups for everything, it is not because you are inferior. It is because you have been made more an orphan than they have.

Lost from yourself

So you Christians, if you're serious about staying Christians tell your preacher, tell your teachers in religion, to help you find yourself; because if you're not managing life and having success at that and you are not contributing anything to your neighborhood, to your environment, you're just living on others who are doing that. You are lost from yourself. There is a saying of Prophet Muhammed that says, "Whoever has known himself has known his G_d, his Lord." Think about that. Man did not come to know the Cause for his existence, the great Creator, called by different names; he did not come to know that by seeking to know that. He came to know that by seeking to know what he is or what she is, or what the family is to do with their life on this planet earth in this material environment.

And the more he worked to know how he can produce and prosper the bigger his mind got. He took on bigger concerns, bigger interests. He had to be responsible for bigger concerns and bigger interests and that expanded his mind and made him want to know how the sky is kept in order like that. And those bodies, what are they? Are they the only light or is there something else up there?

So the working to make his family life better brought so many things of interest into his hands that the interest became so big that it just opened up his mind to the whole universe and then he began to search creation. And as he began to search creation he became a thinker and the thinker became a seer and the seer became a Prophet; and the world became much bigger and much greater.

But now we're living at the end of time. Some people think that the end of time is going to be when the earth is blown up. Why should the earth be blown up? It hasn't done any wrong. We speak of this continent we live on now, the Northern part of it, the United States of America, as the new world, don't we? This is the new world order and it is all over, but we speak of this part that we're on as the new world. South America, America, and parts of these continents that were discovered, they are called the new world and we see a new kind of way of living.

Mother Earth births natural men and women

It is not like it was when they were in Europe. This is the American way of living here and that old world is gone. So for the American citizens that old world is gone and we are in a new world. The earth stays as it is but how we live on it changes according to our own spirit and interest. G_d is not telling you the earth itself is going to be destroyed. It means the way you perceive the earth is going to be destroyed. The earth in your mind is going to be destroyed and the environment that you made is going to have to change. And for some of you on this planet earth your whole environment is going to have to be erased, total destruction. And it is going to have to be made all over again to respect the life that Mother Earth gives birth to.

Mother Earth never gave birth to somebody freakish like most of these people we're looking at on television, on the streets, etc. Mother Earth births natural men and women, industrial minded people, workers, producers, loving to come home after the day's work and socialize; love one another, enjoy each other's company, go to sleep and wake up feeling they are safe and secure in a home of human beings. And now right in your own family you don't know whether you're going to wake up with a human being or a damn alien who may come at you with a hatchet or something, or with a knife, or a gun. We're lost. We all have become orphans.

Where is our first father? It is written, "Unless the children's hearts be turned to the father". You are thinking that is G_d. No, it means the original nature, your first father who G_d awakened to do His work on this earth, in this earth, and produce for generations to come. Unless the children's hearts be turned to the father and the father's heart be turned to the children, G_d says He will smite the earth with a curse. I want you to know it is smitten. We're living under a curse and we can save ourselves if we will live again; and we're to help you if you need help, to show you how to have life again.

Inheriting the Desert

Regarding inheriting the desert the reference for Hagar and her children is, "We're not going to have any uneducated servant people inheriting our culture. Go make your own". So starting your own culture is just like going to a desert. There's nothing born there yet. The desert has been used as a symbol for the absence of cultural development. In our dictionary culture is more than just entertainment, beautiful environment with flowers and stuff. The strongest element of culture is its true educational sciences, because it is usually the sciences and education based in reality that improves the culture of a people, takes on new growth. You go up in the North where there is very little sunlight, there is not much life up there is there? You do not go there to find all of the beautiful flowers and the luscious farmland that you find in the warmer zones.

All Life Out of Water

Up there at the pole you expect to find the absence of that and it is because of the sun. They get little sunlight up there; long periods of night, short periods of sunlight.

Sunrise like birth of the sciences

So the birth of the sciences is like a sunrise and in time the sunlight favoring that area produces just so many different kinds of growth, as Allah says in Qur'an, beautiful pairs, in beautiful relationships; not just with each other but relationships and the context is community life for human beings; so in relationships to other beautiful growth, politics included. Don't they all support each other? The beauty in the physical environment supports the soul, the spirit and nature of the human soul and it gives beauty to the landscape. The rich and poor like it and the high ups and the low people on the ground, the grassroots, like it and it just forms relationships and all of these contribute to our good social life as citizens.

So the water that G_d addresses when He tells us how He started growth, everything had its beginning in that water. And Genesis says in the beginning there was darkness and the spirit moved along the face of the waters and things started to happen. What Allah gave Muhammed behind that a few centuries afterwards was tied right into that. But instead of saying, "In the beginning there was darkness" and giving that same story, it said everything living had its beginning in water. And then it gives seven levels of light in the Qur'an and it says the water is darkness. Water is darkness and land is light. It doesn't say that. I'm just carrying it further. You don't set a fire in the water. You set it on the land.

4

Man and the Universe

So what is it telling us? That the Garden in Genesis is not talking about a physical spot on earth. It is not even talking about the whole earth. It is talking about the creation, all of it; because in the Qur'an it says the width of it is as the heavens and the earth. So the real help meet, the mate, your wife, is not only the earth, it is the universe.

Man and the Universe

Man and the universe are mates created for each other. It is timeless relevancy. That is excellent. So that is what time it is. Religion and science are coming together. That is what they're saying. That is man and his mate coming together. He's going to get his wife back. Everything has to be seen connected if it is scripture, G_d's revelation. If it is G_d's revelation or communication to mankind it is connected. If it is not connected then somebody has misread it.

"If you had not plowed my heifer"

The Bible talks about Samson who said, "If you had not plowed my heifer you would not have broken by riddle, my secret". His heifer pulls the plow. It is a cow like a bull, oxen, pulling the plow but he said it's his heifer. Why did he say his heifer? It is because this is a young woman. You didn't get an old woman. You got a young woman. But that is all he had to do, get a young woman and it puts his eyes out. They cut his hair and then they put his eyes out. They fired up the fire and put it close to his eyes and blinded him. So getting back to the point, what is it talking about, "Plowed my heifer"? Plowing refers to a garden, farmland, and Adam was put in a garden and given the responsibility for it.

So when you plow it you're making it productive. You are accepting your responsibility for it. And when Allah tells us through Muhammed in the Qur'an that the garden, the space of it is as the width of the heavens and the earth, He is going to give you a garden that you will inherit. That means it is your natural right, it is your nature to have it. It didn't say you will get it as a gift. You will inherit the garden. So that means it is naturally yours. It is yours by nature, your natural property by virtue of your nature. So the whole universe becomes the garden.

Garden of Eden refers to all of creation

So what is it telling us? It is telling us that the garden in Genesis is not talking about a physical spot on earth. It is not even talking about the whole earth. It is talking about the creation, all of it; because in the Qur'an it says the width of it is as the heavens and the earth. So the real help meet, the mate, your wife, is not only the earth, it is the universe. And it is not the mate of your biological body which it is, too, because we are one material creation. It is one consistent whole, the material creation. This is true, literally. But what it is really talking about needs interpretation and that is man's mind was created to digest the universe. And that is exactly what man has been trying to do and he has made a lot of progress. You know digest does not only mean with your mouth, but you have *Reader's Digest*. They say, "Food for thought". That will let you know this world is not crazy. It's not ignorant. It is not backwards, we are. That is why they have the world. They have the light. *Reader's Digest*, that is where we want to be, not cannibals. Shaitan made the garden, the innocent garden that G_d gave us, not innocent anymore. But the way G_d brings the children here you're working with that light. You're working with the kinder garden, praise be to Allah.

No veil between G_d and His servant

Allah says, "Nothing is between Me and My servant, not even a thin veil". And in al-Islam there is no priesthood, because Allah said that nothing, no mediator, is necessary. "You want to help My servants? Good, I will reward you for being a good servant. But if you don't help them they are still going to get My communication, eventually, because there's nothing between Me and My servant, not even a thin veil." And that is referring to Moses. He spoke to G_d but behind a veil.

He spoke to G_d, but behind a veil and in his ascent up the mountain he spoke to Him by reference. G_d spoke to him and gave him a reference, but not directly. And in Judaism Moses spoke to G_d behind a partition like a veil and when the priest takes your confession there is a little veil between you and him and that is from the same thing, "You can't see My face. Don't talk to me directly," because he is supposed to be representing G_d. And higher government leaders they are all the same. A lot of them even if they speak to you they have someone for you to speak to, not directly to them.

Man and the Universe

G_d's Presence in the Material World

I have come to understand G_d's presence in the material world and I don't teach this because it will border on some other religious teaching more than on ours from the first appearance of it. But I'm convinced about what Allah says of Himself. He says the whole sky, He controls it. He has it in one hand and the earth in the other hand. That means the works of man's life in one hand and the works of the natural creation in the other; that He has both of these in His hand. It means in His control. So that means to me, especially now that I have seen more evidence, but even before I received this kind of evidence that I receive now in my life every day. I said to myself, "You know, this is my body. My body is my body and my body is an influence in my life, my intelligence inside of it. Even when I'm asleep my body won't roll off the bed. It stays on the bed. And if I've got something pressing on me, my body wakes me up, lets me know it is time to get up. "You got enough rest. I got enough rest. You get up and go on and take care of your business." That is my body.

He is present everywhere

And if a little gnat crawls on the tip of my toe and the shoe and socks are off, I know it. And it is no big thing for me to take care of that little gnat, saying, "Oh, a little gnat is on my toe". I can continue to write my speech. He is not worth me giving my attention to. He is not harming me. So I said to myself, "Now, how much more is G_d in control of the universe that He made with his two hands?" And He is present everywhere. This is the teachings. He's present everywhere. If He is present everywhere it doesn't burden Him. He is present outside of everything He is the Hidden and the Exposed. In English it means, "He is the Apparent and the Hidden, huwal dhahil wal baatin. He is what shows. He is what appears before your eyes and what does not appear before your eyes". Baatin means that which is inside. What is another word for stomach? In Arabic, it is, "Butnun" which comes from, "Baatin", and it is inside of your body; that is, the interior. This is your stomach. What is in there is the interior. So it is about center of the whole structure. So for the inside, in Arabic, it comes from the word, stomach. It's, "Huwal baatin, He is the Hidden." But it also means, "He is the Interior". He is the Exterior and the Interior, "Huwal dhahir wal baatin".

Thoughts for Searchers

G_d uses whole creation

So the Qur'an says, "Whichever way you turn there you will find the face of G_d, wajul laah". So, don't worry about East and West. In case you are out and can't find the direction, you have no compass, pray to G_d. Don't say, "I don't know which way to turn". Pray to Him, for whichever way you turn there you will find the face of G_d. It means you are facing Him no matter which way you are looking. And He is the Exterior and the Interior.

So that brought me to see G_d as really existing within His creation, all of it, no matter how far it extends into space, or no matter how far space extends. We don't even know that concept. That is a mystery. Space is a mystery. It is a mystery because you can't come to the end of it. You cannot even imagine the end of it. There is nothing in the human imagination to imagine the end of space, because whatever you imagine, that is space. It is occupying space. Allah says, "Think not that your creation is a bigger thing than this creation of Mine".

So I know just as we use our body and more so because we are limited, like we use our body and like we are conscious of our body, G_d uses the whole creation, universe, all this space, and it is no burden on Him at all. Our body is a little burden on us to know what is happening, to take care of it and everything. It is a little burden, maybe a big burden for some people if they get some trouble in their body. But just for ordinary functioning the body is such a small burden that it is serving you and you are not even conscious that it is serving you. Like my hand (moving), I am not conscious of that. It's doing that automatically. Eyes batting, breathing automatically and everything is no burden. And it (the Qur'an) says, "Allah manages the heavens and the earth and it causes Him no fatigue. And He does not need to rest from anything". It says, "He neither slumbers nor sleeps". So it says, "No just estimate have they made of G_d". In their effort to try to perceive Him in His totality, no just estimate have they made of Him.

Man and the Universe

G_d was there all of the time

My experience made me understand where the Christians are really coming from when they say, "Christ is my personal savior." I know both the way I see it and the way they see it. But the way I see it is that G_d is ever present. He's with everything He created and He is with humans more than He is with anything else He created, because He created humans to extend His creation. So He is with us, personally, all the time. And the more we get in accord with His Will for us, the more He manifests His presence inside of us. But He was there all the time.

In the Qur'an it says, "When My servants ask about Me tell them I'm near." That means, "I have always been near. Let them know they are screaming out thinking I'm eons away in the sky somewhere. Let them know I'm right where they are. They don't have to scream so loud, for if it's inside their hearts I'll hear it, not from their mouths. If they would just whisper inside their hearts, I would hear it". Praise be to G_d.

The Greatest Friend

So really, when you come to know G_d, Allah, the real G_d, Creator of the heavens and the earth that everybody believes in (they call him other names, but really it's the real One they really believe in), when you come to really know Him, then you understand that when you really connect with Him in the way He intended for us to connect with Him, you have found the biggest, the greatest love. You have found the greatest Friend. You have found the greatest wealth in knowledge and in material things. You have just found the greatest of everything possible that you can think of good or of use.

You can get there by indirect routes

Really, you can get there by indirect routes. But if you love Him and you have always been moving in that direction since you were aware of yourself, when you find Him, you know that route was the route that satisfied or brought you nearer and nearer to everything worthwhile that you were seeking. And the people of faith they know Him. You can tell the way they sing. The way they sing about Him you know they know Him.

And David, he really knew G_d, because that was his love. G_d was his love, always. So they say Jesus Christ is Messiah. Was he from the house of David? And what is David? He is love. Isn't that what we should look at? If a guy is coming, telling us he is a Messiah, a revivalist, or something, he's our sheik, shouldn't we ask, "Are you from the house of love?"

The house of light

I'm sure the word, Bethlehem, means house of light. They translate it differently but I'm pretty certain it means, house of light. David and Bethlehem are very important. Bethlehem is a place and David is a human figure, or a human leader, that was formed of love. His son was the prophet, Solomon, and Solomon means peace. The hadith (sayings of Prophet Muhammed) says, "You'll never enter paradise until you have faith and you'll not really have faith until you practice loving one another." So, paradise is the abode of peace, isn't it? So you see how all these things come together and make perfect sense?

Hidden Sciences

This world, this reality is very, very strange. It's not easy to know the real reality, and that's with everything; and it is much bigger than we think it is. But the people of scripture they knew. They mentioned the things like human life and compared it to sand and compared it to dust and different things of the outer world. So they knew the outer world was designed by G_d to show us our reality and even show us what we can't see of our reality. So it gave us guidance or light that would bring us to study our reality as a science, as a scientist, scientifically; look for scientific guidance and answers. "And we would not have found our paths if You had not guided us" (Qur'an).

So we couldn't get it, we couldn't find the paths of the sciences. That's what it is talking about, the paths of knowledge, science, astronomy, mathematics and all these other sciences. "We couldn't have arrived at this if You didn't guide us". And so the great seers and prophets, they saw the need for the mind to meet the matter. Mind and matter must meet and come to a workable relationship where the intelligence, the mind, and heart, are working with the matter, the material universe. And they saw that. And when they saw that they gave credit to Whoever designed this universe, for opening up the matter to them so they would find the paths of the sciences, or the pathways of the sciences.

Mates pure and compatible

We're told in the Qur'an and taught by the Prophet Muhammed, too, that in the next world we shall have mates pure and compatible. They will be mates pure and compatible, of like nature. They will be like our own nature. So if I'm devoted to solving issues for humanity, I should have a wife like that. It may not be in this world, but the next; at least in the next one. "And they shall have "huri'ain, they shall have big wide eyes, open eyes; bright, big, wide open eyes" (Qur'an). And that's what comes when you have, "huri, freedom", when the intellect is free.

It is not talking about any flesh and blood women. No, it's talking about the interest you'll take and the issues you'll engage and they will be of your nature. Isn't that wonderful? Isn't that what we want? Yes, but the world denies you a chance. The world doesn't want to see you develop this that you want to develop, or to have children by this interest. Then man has to suffer until the day comes, the Hereafter. So, that's what it's talking about when 70 virgins are mentioned. Seven is the figure that's used for the hidden sciences.

G_d: A Hidden Treasure

Actually, the human person was a condition that was to happen before even the world could be formed, or have existence. I'm not talking about the world G_d made that was out there long before humans; the world of man, not the world that G_d made. The world that G_d made is nothing but food for man. And He says He made the world for man. For His human creation He made the whole world and He didn't create man for any purpose greater than the purpose of His mercy.

Philosophy had to come before science

What is His mercy for? His mercy is to relieve the burden on life. What life? Human life. There is no burden on any other life. They are not even aware of burden. Everything that hurts them they think it was necessary. It was expected consequences. But man questions consequences and asks, "Why did this happen? And I believe I can change this." This is philosophy. This is religious or scriptural philosophy, but philosophy had to come before science. There was no possibility for science to develop before philosophy developed. Man had to first fall in love with the creation, with G_d's handiworks, and extract from what he was engaging direction for his own intelligence and for his heart. Then, when he was able to do that, pretty soon, he caused the material world to open up and reveal its hidden nature or its hidden operations that you don't see readily. You have to have experiments, etc., to see the inner workings of the material reality.

If man had not fallen in love with G_d he would not have fallen in love with knowledge

So if he had not fallen in love with G_d he would not have fallen in love with knowledge. And if he had not fallen in love with knowledge he would not have fallen in love with G_d. And if he had not fallen in love with something external beyond himself he would never have gotten the pure sciences. This is all truth. And they say, "We would not have found our paths if You had not directed us to them." That is in the Qur'an, in Qur'anic Arabic, "Wa qad hadaakaa subulanaa."

The philosopher says, "G_d is a hidden treasure and He created man because He wanted to be discovered". Does G_d have an ego like humans, like men, that He wants to be known for His high value or divine existence? No. Why does He want to be discovered and why did the philosopher say He is a treasure? He is a treasure because if the human mind, pictured as Abraham, had not searched the existing world of reality to make sense of it, the human being would not have come to the conclusion that this is one system of logic and it is not in conflict with itself. That tells me that it could not have happened without a purpose and without it being designed that way, because I am a mind. I am human and this world feeds my mind and has fed my mind and shown me its unity. So my conclusion is there must be a living Reality behind it that is of a different nature and superior to it that caused it to exist and He did it all for the human being; for His creation, so it would advance and have comforts unimaginable.

Man and the Universe

All life in one progression

So there is the expression, "He created man expressly for His mercy". I had this idea even when I was a young minister. Long before I came to this development I'm in now, I had this mind. I said to myself, "Everything that exists is connected". Right away I started thinking this way on the so-called primitive people and how the Indians and some other primitive people have tried to show the evolution of man and put creatures on a totem pole, showing a progression for life; that all these lives are in one stream, or in one progression. This is a picture or diagram of something showing man's existence with all these other creatures. And man ascends highest on the pole. So thinking philosophically (and that's my nature to think that way) this is a forward step or progression that eventually unfolds into the exact sciences.

Made of the world

So, I'm a man and I think and I have more freedom to think and there are more possibilities for me as a free thinker than it is for any other life that exists. I am made of the world. My living body is made of the world. It came from the world that G_d created and then my mind is influenced by the world G_d created and it comes to life and starts to form and grow, because of it is feeding on the life that G_d created. I eat chicken and when I eat it, it has a chance to rise up to the highest possibility for flesh or matter when it enters my matter. When he becomes a part of my matter, now he is in a situation that lifts him up to the highest possibility for living things. Can't you see how it is justified that G_d give us these things and that He says He created man for the world and the world for man?

World has no real purpose without man

The world has no real purpose without man and man has no real purpose without the world. So if we look to make sense of things we can do it much better than anybody that is trying to do it without the guidance of G_d. In fact, we are the only ones that can do it. Now you tell me I eat and what I eat makes, replenishes, my cells in my body. So do you tell me my flesh body is not chicken? It is chicken, fish, lamb, vegetables, oxygen, hydrogen. This is everything that comes into my body. So if G_d crowns the creation with me everything has been crowned or lifted into the seat, the throne, because of my existence.

If you can't follow that line of reasoning, then look at it this way. They can't appreciate each other and they can't appreciate their own existence, but G_d has created me to appreciate myself and all of them in a framework. That is wonderful and beautiful. So, actually, their reality remains low until man engages them in his thinking. And even if we can't see the material proof that these things have been not put down, but they have been put on earth to be lifted up once they enter man; if you can't see that, then see at least that by themselves they have no real exciting existence or glory. But when they come into the life of man and become a part of his world, they are raised up in importance and value. Their meaning becomes so much greater. So everything is fed into the higher and that is intelligent man.

Whatever you consume becomes your flesh

What about man consuming all animals? Whether he takes them, physically, into his body or not, with his intelligence he's consuming all of them. That concept becomes much more important once man brings their concepts into his vision or into his reading of matter and the world; then, they become so much more important. But that is real. Whatever you consume, if it is consumed by your flesh, it becomes your flesh.

We digest pig with our mind, our intelligence, but we can't eat the flesh. The Muslim can't eat the flesh of a pig or the hog and that has to do with psychological and moral interest. In the history of man's progress as a civilizer he once ate with little moral discretion. He was hungry so he killed something, tore the hide off of it, and ate it raw. He sees something and he's hungry, if he smells it and thinks it won't kill him, he eats it. That is how he survived. But the moral nature in him grew as he grew, as he interacted with the world. It grew to become so strong that he could not stomach his past behavior. Now he wants to wash it up. He wants to clean it and he doesn't even want to eat it raw. He wants to cook it.

So he rises up to a level of moral insight and moral discretion and he looks at a thing that just arouses disgust in him. The behavior is disgusting, pig behavior, pig sound is disgusting and he says to himself, "If I accept this thing into my life as a support for my life and I continue to kill and eat it, it is going to affect my moral nature and my human sensitivities. It is going to affect me, psychologically. I don't like to pass gas in the presence of people eating around me, but this thing passes gas even in the face of the other pig that is eating with it and makes all these nasty sounds. If I eat that thing it is going to affect me, psychologically."

Jesus Christ: The son of light and sciences

Those who fixed up the Bible they had respect for the word of G_d and for people, human life and conditions. But, really, they never said that pig was good to eat. That was the Church interpreting it that way; that Jesus Christ said, "Behold I make everything new". Making everything new, doesn't mean that everything is fit to put in your mouth. A new rat shouldn't be eaten. A new pig is still a pig. But before, he was only a pig. If you understand the science of Jesus Christ, how he is the son of light and sciences in the world, now, when he shines on a pig, it is no more a pig, physically. A pig is a pig as a body of knowledge or science. So that is the newness of the pig. The intelligence has been advanced and lifted up and raised so that it doesn't see only a pig. It sees sciences in the skin, hair, bones, life germs, of the pig. And then he gets science and finds that this is a pig, but it will heal this disease or help this condition in man as medicine from the pig.

An embodiment of knowledge and mercy

That is the newness and, "making everything new". He raises the value of everything previously perceived, because it is no more just a physical animal. It is an embodiment of knowledge and science. The Qur'an says Allah caused everything to be created to broadcast knowledge, or science and mercy. Did mercy come to society before science? Only a little bit, but when the knowledge or science came to society, then great relief came to man, just a whole new possibility for life, comfort, freedom from sickness or diseases, or pain. Transportation, itself, look how it has reduced the pain that people have to undergo to travel to their relatives who live a thousand miles away or less with the modern transportation. That has all been brought about because of man's brain digesting what it engages and then reproducing it for the benefit of society. Knowledge and mercy in the whole creation, everything in it, a speck of dust, no matter how small the material reality is, it all communicates knowledge, or science and mercy.

That is the strongest urge in the soul and intelligence of people. A lot of them don't register it because they are so taken by other things of less importance in their environmental circumstances. So they never are really turned on as an intelligent being or organism that wants to make sense of things, of what it is exposed to, or what is exposed to it. But for those who find or are situated to start developing that way the greatest urge in them is to do just that, make sense of things. When babies come here, girls and boys, it is obvious right away. As soon as they get here they have an interest in what their eyes have opened upon. The mother will be holding them and they will be picking the skin wanting to know, "What is this?" And they don't know that the eye is very sensitive. So, sometimes, they will be picking it and the mother has to pull their hand away, because they are going to stick their hand right under the eyelid where the eye is. They are going to touch that, because they want to know

First appetite to eat mentally

The first appetite in human life is not an appetite to fulfill your physical needs, to eat, physically. It is the appetite to eat, mentally and that is the meaning of Adam, that He created the first man, Adam, meaning the first man was the man that wanted to make sense of the world he was exposed to including himself. So G_d said He taught him the names of all the things. Then the devil came up and offered him an apple. All the animals know to go to the physical things and eat. That is no big deal. But the human being is made to go to the physical thing and eat it with his mind, not with his physical mouth and teeth, etc. Things have to make sense to satisfy the human soul.

I don't know anything that burdens African American souls more than church religion and that is what holds them. That is what has held them up to now. And those who are still held in human conditions they are still in the Church except for a very few. Even those who leave the Church, they don't leave the intelligence of Christian life. They just leave that which turns their intelligence off. The worst off of all the citizens of this country are those who were brought up without knowledge and left with a belief that Jesus Christ, the physical concept that they see that was introduced to them, is a person and is G_d. African Americans, they are the worst off of all the citizens in the United States of America. They are the ones who are so far from the light of intelligence that you don't see any evidence of it being in them at all. They are actually seriously, mentally retarded. I'm not joking!

Minds so empty

When you see them and they talk to you, their minds are so empty of anything that you can respect that much that it almost makes you want to cry, even in their face, or turn and go somewhere and cry. And some of them are not immoral. They have decency. They respect you saying, "Hi, Mr. Mohammed." If they accidently throw something on your car they say, "I'm sorry, I didn't mean to do that", and they will start trying to wipe it off. But they have no spirit to engage you in an intelligent conversation...Some of them work, too. They will go out and work, but they don't have jobs that require much intelligence. They can only hold jobs that require hardly little or no intelligence. They will go to work, come back, eat and laugh with each other, go to bed, get up, repeat it and go back to work...

Religion responsible for lifting up human life

So if we can give people religion that respects their intelligence it will lift the value and worth of human beings in society high enough for Hollywood and police departments, law enforcement and everything to have a high appreciation and respect for human life. It has to come from religion. Religion has been responsible for not only lifting human life up, but responsible also for fixing certain people who have no self-assertiveness enough to meet the challenges of life. It has fixed it so they can't be satisfied with a religion of make believe that keeps them from advancing their life and intelligence. So, ensha Allah (G_d willing), we're going to defeat it. Yes we are. We are defeating it. It is slow, but we're defeating it.

There are other people who feel the same as we feel but most of them don't have faith in the value of the common person created by G_d like we do. Even those who know that language, most of them don't have faith in the common person that we have. The people are performing beneath the standards for human beings and intelligence because they are really ignorant. A few of them are ignorant, retarded. A few of them are impaired; I mean physically, or have psychological problems and are not really in a situation or in a condition to be lifted up in life. But the great many, the big numbers among these people, are really dropouts, who not only dropped out of school, but they dropped out of human life. The great majority of them are victims of a make believe world, starting right in the Church. And if reality can ever be shown to them, they will come into a new mind and a new interest and a new determination to work for their elevation in society. I know that.

How Man Lost Himself

Satan made the world more important than the developer that G_d created, the man. He's supposed to be the developer. Satan made the world more attractive and more important to that man than the plan, or G_d's will for him. He made the world itself more attractive. So when the world captures your imagination and captures your interest then you are separated from your own self. You understand that clearly. But if you are first seeking to know self, that is the first curiosity. Man wants to know, what am I, why am I here? Why do I have this life and nature? Why do I have all these questions? Why do I have this curiosity? Why am I different from the rest of the life? So the first interest for man's curiosity is himself. And he first discovers himself after he partly discovers other things. He has an interest in other things and they take him only so far. The more he gives himself to those things outside of himself the more he's pressured and burdened to look at himself and see what should be his role out here; his role in this reality.

So when the world occupies your time and mind, your curiosity, it takes you away from that need to know yourself and your role in the material world. That is how man lost himself. And Abraham says (in Qur'an), "Surely I have been wrong. I have been oppressing my own self and I confess my faults." It really means "oppressing", in Arabic. It is, "Thalamtu", and it means I turn to G_d, "Guide me because I don't know how to get there. Guide me to the best of morals, for none can guide to the best of morals but You". Praise be to Allah. What a wonderful scripture.

So that is how he got separated. G_d showed the angel, Jibril (Gabriel), His creation and the angel said, "How can anyone go wrong in such a creation?" Then He showed him what the devil had planned for the creation. He put his allurements, his attractions, all over G_d's work. The angel said, "G_d, how can anyone go straight in such a creation?"

"Go on Your Own Recognizance"

The average person worships G_d to promote their own interest and He still accepts their prayers. Isn't that wonderful? Look how wonderful G_d is. He knows they're liars, hypocrites and they are self-deluded. They don't even know they are praying lies. They don't know they're reciting lies. He receives them and blesses them for their good intentions and helps them because they need help and cannot find help inside themselves. It has to come from without. So He helps and blesses them and strengthens them so they can grow and prosper and one day reach that stage where they say, "I have to repent. I have a confession to make. My whole life has been a lie."

The face is a reflector of all that is in the person

They don't know that they are takers and not givers. Abraham, he is the perfect man as a leader, a picture of the type that G_d wants to lead all people and he said, "I have turned my whole self to You". The self is the face, because the face is what registers what is inside. It registers the whole person. If you're sad, happy, if you're deceitful, it registers all in the face. Although other parts of the body can show it sometimes but not like the face. The face is the mirror or reflector for all that is in the person.

So he says, "I have turned my face", meaning I have turned my whole self. That is why they translate it that way, sometimes. It says my face, that is what it literally says, "Surely I have turned my face to You". But they translate it, "Surely I have turned myself to You". And some translations are, "Surely I have turned my whole self to You", and that is true. That is exactly what it means. And what is that to say? That is to say the true achievement or accomplishment for the soul on this path to its perfection or on its path to its destiny is to discover its hidden interest and recognize that, "I thought I was doing this for

G_d. I was doing that for myself. But now that I really correctly understand the reality of G_d and know the reality that G_d has established for me a human person, I don't come that way anymore. I don't have one face for this prayer and another face for my interest in the world. My face for this prayer is the same face that I have when people see me in the world. I have subjugated or subjected myself and all that is of use and benefit and all that represents my life in my want for my life. I have reduced that or subjugated all that to G_d's purpose for my existence. So I have turned my whole face to G_d. I have given my whole self to G_d in obedience to His will and purpose that He established for me as His creation." That is what it is.

Abraham: G_d's friend

So when he did that G_d accepted him and made or called Abraham His friend. That means there are a lot of holy, well-meaning people who are so beautiful in creation and so selfless and are sacrificing so much, "But, did you efface yourself really for Me, or did you efface yourself to impress your fellow man?" Who knows? Saintly people live a saintly life and they enjoy the satisfaction of knowing that people see them as souls who have made an extraordinary sacrifice and by so doing they have lifted themselves up above mortals. "You live on fifty dollars a week. You don't eat too much. You don't go out on Friday nights. Now here you are knocking on the door of My Jannah (My heaven) and your own nature is saying it is closed against you. You cannot come in. Now stand out there and search yourself. If you search yourself long enough maybe you will pray like Abraham did and the gates will open."

Straining to be innocent

Yes, that is what we want and it is not easy. And it does not come without Allah's mercy and without our straining to be innocent. I don't want to be guilty, not before my Lord. I don't want to be guilty of anything. So if you strain to be accepted by your Lord and not to be guilty, if you strain, fall down, you get back up. You leave the path, wake up and find something missing and you start searching; pretty soon you're back on the path. You do that over and over again. The Prophet said in inspired hadith that G_d has a servant that every time he falls by the wayside or sins he remembers to ask his Lord for

Man and the Universe

forgiveness; and he does this over such a long period of time, repeating it, that G_d says, "Go on My servant, you are on your own recognizance. I trust you with yourself. You are a good manager, good custodian, caretaker. I'm trusting you with yourself. I don't have to worry about you. You are on your own."

Have you stopped sinning? No, but you have established a pattern that speaks for your intent to never forget your Lord and for that He trusts you to your own nature and to your own judgment because your judgment is that you should repent if you ever see or recognize that you have done something that you need to repent for. So Allah trusts us with our own authority. Isn't that beautiful? And the judge will say, "You're released on your own recognizance." Now you know they got that from the Qur'an. They got that from the teachings of Prophet Muhammed. I'll bet you if you search the history of that saying you won't find it in there before Muhammed, the Prophet came. You won't find it among any judges, telling a person that he's giving a break to, "Go on your own recognizance. I'm trusting you with your self"

5

Models for Human Society

We're fortunate enough to have a real human being in history and I wouldn't say just Muhammed. Adam was that model before he was deceived. And Abraham was the model and many others. But Adam, Abraham, Jesus, Muhammed, these are all prophets that G_d says are model figures. They're definite figures for us to emulate. Their character and their nature was what G_d gave for all of us. G_d created their nature for all of us.

Models for Human Society

Social Studies begin with a concept of man in society, with a concept of human life and how it should be established in society and that's what al-Islam is. It gives us the concept of the human person and then it gives us the concept of community and that human person is to be established in community. To me that's the beginning of the social sciences. What I mean by that is you have to have some picture of humanity, first, and the human being that you would like to see as a model for society, whether this is an imaginary human being or a real human being in history. We're fortunate enough to have a real human being in history and I wouldn't say just Muhammed. Adam was that model before he was deceived. And Abraham was the model and many others. But Adam, Abraham, Jesus, Muhammed, these are all prophets that G_d says are model figures. They're definite figures for us to emulate. Their character and their nature was what G_d gave for all of us. G_d created their nature for all of us.

And all of us are of that nature. We are that nature. We won't live to see it, maybe, for one reason or another, but all of us, every human being, is created with that nature and it manifests in these models and even without revelation. That's why Muhammed and Jesus Christ are signs that it was done without revelation. He (Jesus Christ) was born in a manger. There was no help for a human being living among animals, born among animals. Where is the help?

Christ and Muhammed in everybody

And his mother didn't help him. According to the Qur'an, when they asked her about him, she pointed to him. So he's a sign of what Muhammed fulfilled and I think the most important thing for us in training students to understand society in the best light for us in society, is to go, firstly, to the creation of man. We have to go to religion and everybody has Christ in them. Everybody has Muhammed in them.

Jesus Christ said, "I in you and you in me (peace be upon him) and Allah said of Muhammed (peace be upon him), "He is a mortal person just like you are". That's to say you're the same, but it manifests in him. So you should look at yourself in Muhammed (peace be upon him). You should look at yourself in Jesus Christ, in Muhammed, in Abraham and in Adam before he slipped. They all were the models that G_d wants all of us to be. Whatever I say I'm not speaking for myself. I'm speaking from my knowledge of Qur'an, Bible and everything. So Jesus in the Bible is the second Adam, isn't he? And he's the son of man, isn't he? He's the son of Adam, but not directly. He didn't have a direct father. But by genealogy in the Bible, you trace his existence back to Adam. It's called the genealogy of Jesus Christ.

No resurrection except on the pattern of Adam

So he's the son of man and the son of Mary. He's the son of man by what reasoning? That Adam was his mother's father and also his father. That's why Muhammed, when he greeted the ones in the ascension (the Miraj), he greeted Adam, "As Salaam Alaikum, my father Adam," to say that, "Yes, I'm from Adam. I'm descended from Adam". And G_d says in Qur'an, "No one dies or is resurrected accept on the pattern of Adam". It means on his life form, that he was a social man of the human race and we all are social. That social life is expressed as political life and whatever else, but we are originally and essentially social beings and the ummah (community) is a social community. That's why we say brothers and sisters.

So these are the things I think you all should be looking at. We should be looking, first, at universality, that al-Islam is universal and it doesn't claim something for people in one location without claiming it in every location on the planet earth. It doesn't establish a reality in a certain country or somewhere. It establishes a reality for the planet earth. And this can be broken down, put on the college level, university level, and it can be broken down to the pre-school level.

Jesus Christ Is Scripture

Prophet Muhammed was such a genuine human being and such a wise human being. He had such faith in the power of righteousness and the innocence of human beings that even with the devil scheming, plotting, and had done it before his time, had everything rigged and set up to bring the people down to defeat the cause of G_d, he had such faith in G_d and mankind that he wouldn't confront them. He was wise. He wasn't only good, but his goodness is what made him that wise. He couldn't be that wise without that goodness, that purity of heart. He didn't confront them. He had no clashes with them. It says in the Qur'an, G_d revealed it, "Our contention is not with you, the people of the Book." He avoided bringing a clash with them like what happened in the Crusades. He avoided that by going around the trouble spots and not addressing them, or not alarming the Christian or Jewish rule. But certain things he outright condemned.

Muhammed did not condemn Christianity

G_d revealed to him to outright condemn some things and made it clear that there was no way to negotiate it. This is the way of G_d and that remains and there is no way for us to meet eye to eye or agree on the belief that a man, Jesus Christ, is the son of G_d. He would not negotiate that. But short of that, he did. They were wise enough to know. Those who really knew scripture, knew Prophet Muhammed was not condemning Christianity. He was condemning those who failed to see correctly in Christianity. So even the Christian order, when they see that he was not really condemning the Christian church or the Christian people as such, but he was condemning their misperception of Jesus Christ and his mother Mary, that they didn't perceive them correctly; they could see his moral excellence and his human excellence and his noble work. They could see all that. So they didn't want to do battle with a man like that. And who knows, perhaps they even thought, "Muhammed, if he lives, maybe he will come to our side. He doesn't see our side, yet." But he did.

Jesus Christ not flesh

When you see their side, the high up in Christianity don't believe like the common people believe. They know that Jesus Christ is not flesh. Jesus Christ is scripture. He is the word of G_d. He is the New Testament. He is the Gospel. They know that. And he is the teacher of the Gospel. He is the Gospel and the spirit, meaning the leader of the Gospel. So he's the teacher of the Gospel and the Gospel is his life, or his body.   So the Qur'an addresses that when it says he was a spirit and word from G_d.

They looked at that and said, "Muhammed is right. Christ is G_d's word and a spirit from G_d". But who can see that except those high in understanding? The masses can't see that. What the masses take is the flesh. They say, "So as much as Muhammed wants us to change, we can't do that. We will lose our masses." Jesus in the Gospel, he took his disciples up to show them something. So he took them up in the mountain and they followed him and here is what they say they saw in the Bible. I'm sure you've read it, some of you who read the Bible like I have. They saw the light of Elijah, the light of Moses and the light of Jesus Christ. There were three lights and they became one.

Qur'an is Jesus personified

So what is Jesus teaching his followers by that? He's teaching them how to rightly identify him, not in the flesh. "I'm going to take you up to see me. I'm not flesh. You have to go up to see me. I'm light. And the light of Moses was a great light. It was the light of how to govern, how to rule; and then the light of Elijah was the light of how to fight, defend, to battle. Elijah did battle with Ahab. He challenged him like Moses. Moses challenged the Egyptian rule, but he's mainly to be seen as a law giver, one who established government. He is the one who represents the light, the science of how to establish government. Elijah is the science how to heal the people. Elijah was a healer of the widow's son. He raised him from the dead. It doesn't mean physically dead. Elijah was the medicine man. He's was a healer. Moses is the government light and Jesus Christ is the moral light, innocence; moral innocence, pure light. When they come together, then you see the Jesus. So Jesus was empowered with the science of government, the science of psychology, how to heal the masses, how to heal the public, the people and also his own moral excellence; his moral innocence. They all came together.

I believe the Qur'an is Jesus personified, the word of G_d. That's scripture. You know it says that the Qur'an is a healing for what is in the breast. So the word itself is Elijah's power. The Qur'an says He would raise up from their brethren one like unto Moses. So Muhammed came to establish government, but not a government like most people think.

New World Leadership

In the Bible the angel, Jibril (Gabriel), shows up to influence Mary, the single person and the plural person. Jesus is the Church and she is the Church, also. He is the Church while he is alive among them. She's the Church when he goes away. He's on the cross and dying and he said, "Behold your mother". That means, "I will not be with you anymore, but the congregation is with you and the congregation has its leadership. You are going to be now in the body of the congregation and not directly in my body or in my message, in my mission", which is his body.

So here are two situations, one while he is living and one after he is gone. Now the one that is in the Qur'an is the one after he is gone. But it is used why? Because that is how he came to be, anyway. He didn't come to be from nowhere. He came to be from a woman, from a congregation. The original Jesus came out of a congregation and he was their leader.

Immaculate Conception an influenced concept

Now the Qur'an wants us to see how he really came about, so it starts off with his mother, not with him. And that's really the one who is first. The mother is before the child, so it starts off with her story. She's told by G_d by the means of an angel that she is going to have a child and she is surprised saying, "How can I have a child?" Like Sarah, she laughed when G_d said she was going to have a child. Mary didn't laugh, but she said, "How am I going to have a child? I'm a virgin. I can't have a child?" And the Holy Ghost overshadowed her. It meant she was influenced with a concept bigger than her reality. It covered her up and blackened her whole existence. It was so much bigger than she was. The concept was so much bigger than she was until her whole existence was overshadowed. And when she had nothing to feed her but the Holy Spirit she became pregnant with child, the Immaculate Conception.

Thoughts for Searchers

Three lights in one

The concept of the Holy Ghost was so much bigger than she was and so much more powerful than she was until it took over, influenced her existence from that point on and she became pregnant with child. She became pregnant with another concept, a smaller concept. And it is an Immaculate Conception, praise be to G_d. Isn't this wonderful? I have been entertaining this for some time and every time I think, "That is so much." When Jesus wanted to tell his disciples, himself, they had been with him, why could they not see him? He goes up in the mountain and shows them the transfiguration; and there he showed himself as light, not as flesh. But he shows three lights; the light of Moses, Elijah and himself. But they were three lights in one. Now where did they get three gods in one? Jesus did not show them three gods in one. He showed them three lights in one; the light of the cultural leader, Moses, and the cultural leader is a political leader in the world.

So it shows the light of Moses who was a cultural leader to bring them into a new culture. They were in a culture that was oppressive in Egypt so he had to take them out of the culture of oppression and bring them into the culture of life, enlightenment and freedom. So Moses is that figure. He is that light. Then Elijah he is a healer. So what heals? Obedience to G_d and the courage to defy authority, that is in the way of G_d. That was Elijah and that heals. The Bible says Elijah healed the widow's son. She does not have a husband, no man. He heals her son and then his life is compatible with those lights. That is why they can become one. They are one light.

Jesus came to establish new world leadership, to take the people out from under the oppressors and to reconcile the spiritual life with the social life. That heals, too. It all means a healing for people who are not having that. So actually what it is saying is that Jesus comes with a light like that of Moses, a light that frees and liberates the people; and he comes with a light like that of Elijah that heals those suffering, because they don't have the light that G_d created them for. That is the widow's son. He healed the widow's son. Elijah had the power to bring down from heaven both water and fire. He prayed at the altar and the fire came down and consumed the offering. And then the water came down and put out the fire. So Elijah had power to pray for water and fire and to have both of those agencies serve him for the purpose that he was put in the world for.

Jesus said, "I come not only of water, but I come of water can and blood". In scripture, blood and fire are the same. It says, "And blood shall come up to the horse's bridle". It is a sign of a great time of killing suffering, great tragedy. The war is going to be so terrible and blood is going to flow up to the horse's bridle. That is in the Bible. It is called blood in the New Testament. But in the old days, in the Old Testament it was fire. So that which was fire before Jesus Christ becomes blood in the time of Jesus Christ.

In the Bible everything begins from water

You don't read about any fire getting anybody in the New Testament. It just speaks of what the Old Testament said warning them of the consequences. Why? Because blood has become the term now that holds the meaning and not fire. But both of them are still true. The Bible, Old Testament, talks about the world being destroyed by fire, but it says blood is the life of the body. Now blood is the life of the body and plagues came upon the people in the Old Testament and one of the plagues was that the water was turned to blood.

In the New Testament that is not a plague. That is a blessing. In the Old Testament turning the water into blood was a curse. Why? It was a curse because they were seeing fire as wisdom and seeing blood as human passion. Fire was wisdom, blood was human passion. So you turn the spiritual life into social passions. That is a punishment for the people because now they are going to be on their own social life and not on the spirituality that G_d revealed. Everything begins from water in the Bible. It did not say the water turned red; just plain water and the light appeared in the water and the world was generated. In the Old Testament water is light and blood is passions.

They tricked the savage rulers

The New Testament kind of reverses all of that, whereas, blood is not passion. What is the New Testament doing? It is deceiving the dictatorships of the world, saying, "Now, you think you understand what is going on here. You don't. The fire has become blood and the water has become stagnant spirituality. This man is going to change this dead water into living wine." This is the beauty of it. They tricked the savage rulers so when they looked at it and saw it, they said, "This is good". They said, "He (Jesus Christ) wants to take care of our tired and worn out people. We need help. Let him give this to them. It is not going to hurt us." That is what they thought. But the following who became the leaders got the insight from the teacher. Jesus taught them how to look at that.

The world could not see it so they let them work when they got the people with them. Like Jacob, he made a deal with Laban. He said, "All the cattle that come out reign streaked will be mine" and Laban agreed to it. So they said, "This man only wants your tired and worn out people who cannot do you any good any way. They are donkeys. He can ride this donkey for you". So they bought it. They gave their masses to Christianity and that took a lot of trouble out of their hands. And what the Christians were doing was selecting them very carefully to educate them, as many as they could educate. Finally, their leaders ascended to the throne. They were better qualified and the whole so-called heathen nations of that area converted to Christianity. Once they learned what was happening it was too late. Already, their best minds were Christians, but by secrecy.

Blood is both fire and education

They were hiding what they were teaching and they came into power. So the New Testament blood is both fire and education, fire and teaching, wisdom. It is fire because it is wisdom in the social life, nature and social passion of mankind. That is where its wisdom comes from. So it is fire that enlightens, too. It is a light and it warms you. Social teaching will warm you up like fire, passions. They warm you up. They make you spirited and the more you put air into fire the bigger and more powerful it gets. So they put G_d's Spirit into the passions and the more excited the passions become it warms up the world. That is Jesus Christ. He was blessed to have that. He was blessed with the Holy Spirit and it was not given to go out on the waters. That is the way the world started, on the water. The Holy Spirit, here, is to be fired into the social life and passions of the people. So he is not only of water. He is of water and blood.

An Overriding Aim

Prophet Muhammed was born among people who had irrational faith. Their religion was irrational. They worshipped idols. But he was not of them. He was of a special class and that class was the intellectuals of his day, in his tribe, the Quraish, who believed in the excellence of nature. They already believed that and they were called the hunafaa, the plural of haneef. And then when Muhammed was shown the path and he knew Abraham in the scripture was shown favor as a father, leader for all the people, he identified their belief-the hunafaa-as the belief of Abraham. That's the only thing that was missing in the hunafaa. They didn't have revelation. So when he got revelation, then he understood that revelation complemented the hunafaa's identity as a creation, human creation; that it complemented it. So then he saw that to purify that nature we need revelation. Though we are striving for excellence to purify it we need G_d to reveal to us. So G_d gave him revelation to show him how to purify his nature. But he already believed in the excellence of his nature.

The excellence of man's nature

But revelation showed him that really the way to continue the life of the excellence of his nature he needed revelation. He needed G_d to open up the whole world to him. So when Allah says in the Qur'an that it is the deen of origin, deen al-fitrah, His religion of origin, the originality or the origin that this human society is fashioned upon, then Muhammed understood that it was the haneef, that nature, that Islam came to complement; and that, really, the pattern that Allah had designed the Qur'an to fit is really the haneef, the excellence of man's nature.

Creation has an overriding aim

Abraham is the father. He's the father because he was before Muhammed and the first one to question the external reality, looking for G_d. He came to the conclusion that G_d is none of this. That G_d is the One that designed it. And how did he come by that? He was from among the hunafaa, the plural of haneef. He believed that his creation had an overriding aim. Maybe it would commit an offense here or maybe it would disgrace its value here or there, but it has an overriding aim and it's going to come out in somebody. So, it came out in the hunafaa, that group that he gravitated toward, or they gravitated towards each other. Muhammed, the Prophet, believed there is an overriding aim that originates in nature; that it was nature; that it was the dominant nature. And he believed that everything created had that same nature. But it's not called by that name. Only for humans it's called haneefah, or hunafaa.

The Mercy of G_d

When asked about his life and how he succeeded without being overcome by sin, Prophet Muhammed said it was because of the Mercy of G_d. The same goes for everybody else, because of the Mercy of G_d. Now why does the Mercy of G_d work for him but it doesn't work for so many others? It worked for him because his spirit was always to do the best, to do the correct thing and to be the best in his character and conduct. He was always truthful and trustworthy, so he earned Allah's Mercy; and that Mercy was to free all people, "Rahmatan lil 'aalameen, mercy for all the people", because of one person. Didn't the Bible say if there's just one in the city He wouldn't destroy it? The Qur'an says, "Surely your life and your death is as one soul". So because there was that one, all of humanity got mercy. So how is all of humanity going to get mercy without revelation? That's why G_d revealed to him.

Two arrows shot from one bow

Now, that's not the end of this logic, because he said when they asked him what accounts for you being saved from that, he said, "The Mercy of G_d", the same as for everybody else, the Mercy of G_d. So what do I see in that? Because he was truthful and trustworthy, that being in his nature was also mercy from G_d. G_d knows that this creature that was formed from his mother and his father, this creature wants no evil, wants no wrong. G_d knows in the beginning. G_d says, "Here's a soul that wants nothing but Me. He wants Me. He wants to serve Me. He wants to find Me and serve Me. So, I'm going to make it easy for him. I'm going to be the Protector of his purity." So Allah protected his purity and put him in circumstances that would aid that. So Allah was working with him as his Lord and Creator right beside him from the day he was conceived in his mother to the time he died; like two arrows shot out of one bow.

Models for Human Society

Don't need everybody to save human society

Yes, so you know Allah knows. None of us, no one, can be without sin. They all-I'm talking Bible-are sinners. Was Jesus Christ a sinner? But it says all are sinners. Did it say Jesus Christ was a sinner? No, it's speaking of him, that all other than him were sinners. And why was he not a sinner? In the language of the Bible it was because he was the son of G_d, a spirit and a word from G_d. How could he sinful? Now, for Muhammed, I already explained to you how he couldn't sin. So we all are human with these human limitations and without the intervention of G_d, Himself, we all would be lost. Yes, we don't need everybody to save society. All we need is one soul. One soul started it and one soul can redeem it, or bring about redemption, earn redemption.

6

Scriptural Reasoning

This (America) is modern day Egypt. Culture-wise, that is exactly what it is. This is no mythological connection I'm making. This is reality. They planned it that way, for America to be modern day Egypt.

Scriptural Reasoning

Jesus Christ said he'd knock the dust off of his feet. If they reject him he'll leave the town. It says, "But pity on them if he knocks the dust off his feet". It means he was lifting up the people who didn't have any material establishment. They were like dust and could be blown or taken away by the breath or by the spirit. So they were not going to let him carry the dust of the people, of the poor and ignorant people. He said he'll knock it off, leave them there with them; and it would be worse than Sodom and Gomorrah what would come behind him. Yes, that's what religion does. True religion, it goes after the suffering people and tries to take them off of the ground and put them in a better position to make something out of their lives, do something with their lives. And if you prevent that kind of a messianic leader or that kind of preacher from doing his work then that nation leaves them without someone to gather them and do something with their lives will be threatened by those people, that element in their society. And eventually, it will cause their downfall.

The spirit crowd

So, the feet, are the spiritual people…and it's the spirit that holds up everything. The poor people, they are in the feet and the rich people are in the money. Yes, the spiritual teacher, he gathers the poor people. They respond and he gathers them and they are like dust on his feet. His foundation was not dust. His foundation is spirit. Jesus Christ was the spirit of G_d and a word from G_d. So his spirit is very strong and also with the spirit is faith; faith, spirit, and the word of G_d which guides him. And that's in the foundation. But now if he goes out of that foundation and the dust goes away and is left back there with the people they're in serious trouble. And that's what the Bible is saying, that his coming and taking up the cause of the poor and the ignorant people is what spares great nations, or great powers and it does. But they've always had a way of managing the spirit crowd, or those people who have spirit but not knowledge and guidance.

"Why have you struck me these three times?"

The ancients have always had a way to contain and hold the masses. Baal is one of them. G_d calls it Baal in the Bible, B-a-a-l. And you know Baal was riding the donkey, until the donkey saw an angel with a flaming sword, a messenger with a flaming sword, or with the word of G_d that's like a flaming sword; a sword that lights up. And it doesn't only cut, but it lights. It's a light, also. It cuts and slays, but it's a light, also. That's the word of G_d. So the donkey saw the angel holding the flaming sword in the pathway, in the way that it was traveling on with his master on his back. So the donkey said, "Why have you struck me these three times?" It says he spoke with a man's voice, not a donkey anymore. The donkey spoke with a man's voice and he said, "Why have you struck me these three times?"

"Only one!"

Now that's answered in Bilal. Bilal was a slave to his master and he was refusing to obey his master. That's asking his master, "Why have you struck me these three times? Why have you put my whole future in slavery, my flesh, my mind, and my spirit?" So his way was just to protest slavery and for doing that his master put him in the hot sun and Jesus was put in the heat, too, wasn't he?

So they put him in the hot sun and then put a heavy stone on his back and they thought that that would make him break and decide to give up his interest in Prophet Muhammed's call to Islam. But when he couldn't speak, he just held out one finger. He was so miserable he couldn't even speak. He just put up that one finger, telling the one who insists he believe in more than one G_d, that he still believed in one G_d. He said, "Ahad, only One!"

And finally, one from the Muslim side, a friend of Prophet Muhammed, Abu Bakr, came and paid his ransom, which shows that the master's interest was in money. The reason why he had a slave as a slave was because a slave was giving him money. So when the money came in a big enough amount, he gave up that slave. After all, he had lost him anyway.

So Bilal is actually the answer. Prophet Muhammed knew this. He's the answer to the scripture that portrays the poor and ignorant people as a donkey and that one day the donkey will speak with a man's voice. So the call to Islam doesn't accept that the people be ruled through their spirit, or by psychology; but that they be free to be educated; that education is the answer.

Modern Day Egypt

This (America) is modern day Egypt. Culture-wise, that is exactly what it is. This is no mythological connection I'm making. This is reality. They planned it that way, for America to be modern day Egypt. They say, the Promised Land. They acknowledge that. So we can reason then, that this is modern day Jerusalem, because Jerusalem is supposed to be the Promised Land. But it is not modern day Jerusalem. The Jews were in Jerusalem and the Bible says, "Take your child and flee to Egypt". So it is not Jerusalem, it is modern day Egypt. It has the same effect. It just overwhelms the poor man.

The first time I went to New York City and passed by those tall buildings and looked up, I got dizzy. It overwhelms you and that is what Cairo means. It means, it overwhelms you. You know the attribute of G_d, the Subduer, is taken from the name, Cairo. Cairo is Qahera and subduer is al Qaaher. And it is no accident that the name, Cairo, was taken from that attribute of G_d. That is to say the mightiest subduers you have in the history of mankind were the Pharaohs of Egypt. But G_d is the real Subduer, because He made Pharaoh and all of his efforts nothing but a sign left for you to remember what happened. The word in English for the Arabic word is nikal and it has a lot to do with nickel.

Secrets of your life in the crib

Nickel is metal and it is five cents. So the Arabs use the word nikal and it came into our language as nickel. And it is a very hard metal that looks to be pure. It looks to be silver but it is not pure. And that is what the culture of ancient Egypt was. It was very difficult to decipher. So nickel was in their language but now we say kryptonite. That is made up. There is no kryptonite. You can't get it out there in the metal field. It is made up to say it is very difficult. It's very hard to manage and it came from the crib (krib-to-nite). They have the secrets of your life in the crib. That is what they managed Superman with; the evil ones. It is supposed to have come from the planet he came from up there in outer space somewhere.

A Living Spirit

History says that Ham is Egypt. We know these are only figures, not true people. These are depictions of a disposition in people, major dispositions in the soul and nature of people that make them appear to be silly, given to too much fun. Some are too serious, too critical and one is the very beautiful image of a human being. He wants to be at peace. His nature is to be at peace. So these are the three sons of Noah and Ham wasn't cursed, directly. According to prophecy or scripture the curse that he earned fell upon his children and they were the people of Canaan land, Canaanites.

Descendants of Canaan (canines) have been barking

Now if you listen to that word, Canaanites, you can almost hear canine and most of the descendants of Canaan have been barking for the last 15 or 20 years, whenever they're excited. It can be at a dance, or a movie. You see how you're manipulated to do things that shame you in the eyes of the intelligent, learned people of the world? It is time to break that. Professor Fard left something that went into Elijah and it went out of Elijah into Wallace D. Mohammed and we are not ready to break it, get rid of it forever.

There is the story of Prophet Noah being seen in his nakedness, drunk and his son, an African (remember Egypt is in Africa) behaves in a shameful way, showing ignorance instead of intelligence and laughs at the condition of his father. So for that he's cursed and it does not fall immediately on the African people. But it falls later upon those who are lesser evolved culturally and politically, the Canaanites. But those Canaanites were superior in iron work. This is history and scripture. Do you think that left us, just like the tendency to give ourselves to too much fun or fun life is still with us? The iron skills we had for iron making and ornamental designs never left us. You go to the Carolinas and you will find that the African Americans there are known for beautiful iron works; just like the Palestinians were builders in ancient time and are still used by Israel, those that live there, to build for them. Palestinians are the more prided builders of Israel.

Scriptural Reasoning

Bilal type is also genetic

We are born with certain things in our genes from our fathers or from the first human type, Adam. But if over long periods of time, generations, a particular people give themselves to certain interests, occupations, eventually, that spirit will go into their children and will be seen manifested in their children. And not only the spirit will go into their children, but their children will be easily adapted to the same jobs or same occupations that their forefathers were adapted to. It will be in their genes. We're great wood carvers, did you know that? Africans and African American people work great with wood carving, designing and making things of wood.   It came from our ancestors and it has survived in our genes. It is genetic. So this Bilal type is also genetic. We're not Africans anymore, but we're certainly Bilal. We haven't stopped being Bilal. We're still Bilal. We still are easily moved by sadness and joy, easily moved by the extremes of them. We're the ones like the black mama who in Africa saw a white woman who couldn't nurse her baby and she goes to the white woman and says, "May I take your baby? I'm nursing my baby." And she nursed the baby of the white woman right along with her own baby.

Jovial extremes lead to adult juvenile delinquents

So these extremes are in us and they are beautiful, but extremes need to be controlled. You say, "Those people, they like jubilation. They like to be happy. They are jovial." What about juvenile? That is where they'll go if you don't check it. You will go to an extreme where your whole people, the grownups, will become juvenile. And the next thing is juvenile delinquency. And when you see all our boys out there, some of them 30 and 40 years old, still acting like they're teenagers on the corner, having no interest in getting a job and taking care of a family, they have become juvenile delinquents.

Too much fun making

It is because the whole race has given itself to too much fun making, have burned out the intelligence of the brain with too much fun making. This is very serious what I'm telling you and once you know what caused your condition then you should just automatically stop behaving that way, showing the people, "I'm not of that mind and spirit any more".

So Bilal in the scripture carries Baal upon his back. I'll just say he carried having a ball upon his back, just always having a ball. He carried that upon his back and his own soul was riding him and he stops. He sees an angel in the way, in the path ahead of him, standing, blocking the way. And according to the scripture the angel had a flaming sword in his hand. Now even a donkey would stop and start being serious minded if he saw something like that. So when he saw that he asked his rider, "Why have you struck me these three times?"

First life is in the flesh

Now I don't want to spend too much time on this but life starts in the physical body, the flesh. When a baby is born from its mother it has no life anywhere except in its physical body. It becomes conscious of our world then life starts in the mind and in the soul. Before that time there is no life except in the physical flesh. The baby is not even expressing itself yet and sometimes they don't wake up automatically on their own. The doctor or somebody has to strike the flesh to get them to breathe air and let it come in. Once they breathe air on their own now he's a live child. He's a living human. But before then he's not and if he does not breathe air he dies. What do they say? He was still born. It means dead, he died. He didn't live. He never came into a life as a human person.

The first life is in the flesh before even the conscious comes on. Then life comes into the mind; so first in the flesh, then in the mind. And if the mind hangs around long enough that particular child is going to develop its own spirit. So now the child is a living flesh, living mind, and living spirit. That is the three. So the donkey says to his master, his rider, which is his own ignorant soul, "Why have you struck me these three times?" No answer came but the donkey had stopped being a donkey. It says the donkey spoke with a man's voice, not with a donkey or animal voice and said, "Why have you struck me these three times?"

Seven Locks

G_d says in the Qur'an He feeds us from the earth and from the skies and He says he gives every living thing its needs, provisions, in four measures. So four from the earth and four from the sky and then they are reconciled like, "Thy kingdom come"…" The language is consistent all through the scripture. Ezekiel said he saw four living creatures go up, ascend, to the heavens, with the face of a man; human creatures, a wheel in a wheel. Now you take one circle and put it on top of another what do you have? What does it look like? A circle on top of a circle is an 8. You take one square and put it on top of the other square and what is that? It is eight. And after you have been fed what do you say? I ate (eight). It is no accident that those sounds are harmonious, they are homonyms.

"If you had not plowed my heifer"

I told you the cow is nothing but a scholar. And Samson said to those who captured him and put his eyes out, "You would not have solved my riddle if you had not plowed my heifer. You got my secrets from my students, my scholars that I made". So the woman who was there with Samson, Delilah, that is his helper and she was very attractive. It meant his scholars who received divine guidance and wisdom from him and in the eyes of the world they were so attractive. And they will be put into one figure called Delilah and Delilah, his own students, prepared him for the takeover. She cut his seven locks off.

They used her. That is right. Those are his students. Those were his choice students. And they were the ones who gave the secret of his power to his enemies; through them. They are put into one figure but those are his students. And how do I know this? I know this because he told his enemy, "You would not have broken my riddle if you had not plowed my heifer" and his heifer was Delilah.

Hair as a metaphor

She cut off his seven locks and "locks" implies secrets. So it was hair. But the hair represents his secrets. And how is the hair secret? The hair is secret because the hair is a metaphor. It is not real, either. The woman is not a real woman. The hair is not real hair. But the hair is a metaphor and if you see the metaphor then the metaphor refers you to or suggests the language that you need to really understand what it is saying.

Now your skin is for touch in you, but hair makes it more sensitive. It makes the sensation stronger. If a little gnat flies onto your hair you know it. So it is like communication lines that go to the skin and a little bit under the surface of the skin to the very nerve endings. So you just do that and you feel it. Just touch it lightly and you feel it in your skin.

Well, the more penetrating sensation, or the stronger sensation, stronger than the natural, the ordinary is what you get naturally at birth. So these are feelings that become worldly. You use them so much in interacting with each other the skin becomes the feeling that the world gives you. But the hair is under, or the inherent ability to sense what is going on is under. And it is funny. Around the world, even among the American Indians, they thought that if you take the hair you steal the soul. So they scalped the white man and thought that they took his soul. Superstition, but originally it had science in it and they lost it. There are people who had it. I guess they went astray. They just lost the connection and became just superstitious.

Inherent intelligence

It is obvious that the hair represents a deeper sensation or a deeper awareness. Animals, dogs, bigger animals, when they do not know what to do and they are in danger, the hair raises up on their backs, on the back of the neck, mostly. That is that deep sense that is telling them, "Don't run up to this thing, you might regret the consequences and it will be too late." He says, "Come on, show me what you've got. I am not running up there to get it."

So it is a deeper caution, deep-rooted caution, or your inherent intelligence. That is what it is. So he was sharing that with his students. The senses that we got that we work with in the world, they are not as beneficial as what G_d works with. G_d works with our inherent nature and our inherent intelligence. And when He wakes it up, then you have a special man in the leader. Hair is your spiritual sense and this (hairless skin) is a social sense or social sensitivities and sensibilities. And this (hair) is spiritual sensitivity and sensibilities, always the two go together.

Now, someone might ask, "Did the students willingly give up what he gave them? Were they conscious?" Well, did Judas willingly do that to Jesus? Some people will sell you out, that is all there is to it. They see something bigger than you, much bigger. They are impressed by it and they do not have the insight that the leader has.

The Snake in Scripture

In Genesis of the Bible, not in the Qur'an, in the beginning the only living creature outside of Adam and his wife was a snake. He made all of the others, but in the garden the scene is Adam, his wife, the trees and the snake; and it was a snake that approached them. And who was the snake? In the Qur'an it is Iblis and G_d said to them, "Get down into the earth". The Bible says that the serpent was told to, "Get down into the earth in the dust, to crawl on your belly". The Qur'an says the same thing, but it's just that he was told to get down into the earth. All of them were told to get down into the earth.

A cold-blooded creature

The serpent appears in the Qur'an but not in the garden. He appears in the story of Moses, where he is told to cast his rod and he cast his rod and his rod appeared in every respect to be a snake, moving. So getting back to the snake, if you look at the human body, at the anatomy, you'll see the brain connecting to the ganglia and down the spine, all the way to the end like it had a tail once. The end of it looks like a little tail. So really what approached him in the garden was a heartless intelligence that didn't have anything to work with but the brain and the nerve center that goes down; that's all. And it looks like a snake with a big head.

So that's really where their information is coming from. The information is coming from the brain going down. You take the brain and the nerve line that goes all the way down to the end and it looks like a snake, a big-headed snake. That's exactly what it looks like. So that's the picture they're giving of the devil, Satan, the intelligence with no human feelings, no heart, no human heart.

He does only what his intelligence bids him to do. He has no regard for human sentiments or heart or anything.

He can't see his evil, because he has nothing to register anything else but intelligence. He prides himself in his intelligence. He despises humans, typical humans, because the typical human lets his heart interfere with his intelligence. It's the heart that feeds the whole body, including the brain. A snake is a cold-blooded creature.

G_d speaking even when Moses is speaking

I said earlier the snake in the Qur'an doesn't appear again till much later, not in the genesis. It doesn't appear in the genesis. It doesn't appear in the beginning. When G_d said, "Get you down from here", there's no mention of any snake. That was the beginning, the genesis. But it appears in the life of Moses and he (snake) is in the staff that the people use. He got into the staff. And we understand the staff by how Allah, or G_d, brings Moses to realize what his staff is. But Allah is speaking even when Moses is speaking. Allah asks a question and then Moses speaks for Allah to tell Allah what Allah wants to bring out. He says, "What is that that you have in your hand? Oh, this is my staff. What do you use it for? Oh I use it to beat back the brush when I'm making a path through the brush."

The science of the culture

So his staff opens a path up through the brush in the woods. That's what he is doing with it, opening up a path so he can go his way through the brush, through the woods. So that's the science of culture and the devil has gotten into it. That snake of the Genesis has gotten into the science of the culture and is regulating the people's life through the science of the culture. So who's making that path for him (Moses)? The devil. Who shows him how to go through the woods? The devil. I hope it's clear.

"Get you down from here"

In Chapter 53, verse 39 of the Qur'an it says, "Wa an laisa lil insaani illaa maa sa'aa. There is not for the human person anything except by striving". If you don't strive or struggle you won't have anything. A snake is called also by the Arabic word, "'asaa". Why is the snake called this? The snake is called this because it appears that other creatures, not formed like it have a much easier life than the snake in terms of its movement, how it travels, how it transports itself; because it transports itself with its skin. It transports itself with its skin and it is seen as a very difficult life.

But what are the wise referring to and why did they name the snake that? "And He taught Adam the names of all things". They named the snake that because what they were talking about, really, was not a snake. What they are talking about is really the human spirit. If you depend on your skin; more correctly, or more pointedly, if you depend on your sensitivities, your feelings, to carry your life, you live a miserable life! That's a difficult and miserable life. Intelligence, rational insight, etc., should be transporting you, with your heart, with your good heart. But if your skin is transporting you, you're like a snake. Do you see how they use these figures to describe the human being? So it's not really the snake, it's a human being. And it says (in Qur'an), "Get you down from here into the earth". So the Bible says to the Shaitan (Satan), "Be a serpent, biting the dust for all of your life, for all of your existence". So it means that he was cast down into the earth to be a serpent.

Shaitan (Satan) moves with feelings, not intelligence

So what does that tell us about the Shaitan, then? It tells us the Shaitan doesn't move with intelligence. He moves with his feelings. And isn't that what we see when he says (in the Qur'an), "You made me better than him? I'm better than him. You made him of mud fashioned into shape, stinky mud. And You made me of fire that gives up no smoke. I don't pollute the air; clean fire. My fire is clean." But his fire was not clean, because in the Bible, all through the Bible, especially when it's referring to sacrifices and fire, what makes the sacrifice acceptable is that the smoke comes from the thing you're burning, or cooking. And the smoke is called a savor, a sweet savor, fine savor, a delicious smell that goes up into heaven from cooking, roasting, or the burning of the fire. And you know they didn't cook, like we do today. It was all barbeque. Our methods came much later.

"I repent nothing"

So the flame and the heat is hitting the meat, making it smell good and the smoke goes up. And they saw the smoke as impurities and the spirit and the impurities coming out but made nice by fire; made nice and made into a good smell. And the animal that smelled bad, if you cook it, it smells good. So they used all of these things. They used the language to say something about their own souls, what is happening to their own bodies, to their own souls, to their own life. So he was boasting that he gave up no smoke, meaning that under heat, "I repent nothing", because the sweet smell is repentance. They identified the nice smell as repentance. When you're under heat or burning you repent your sins. If your disposition is correct, you repent your sins.

The smell of repentance

So the smell was seen as the smell of repentance, true repentance. And another word for repentance would be conforming and conforming would be obeying. And Allah says, "Nothing reaches Me; not your blood, not your sacrifice, only your obedience"; or, only our repentance, you could say. You see how the Bible is saying one thing and the Qur'an is saying another, but actually, when you look at it, in essence, they are saying the same thing.

People think their wealth makes them bigger

Bakhelaa means stingy or miserly. The translation in Qur'an is, "He who was greedy or miserly and thinks himself self-sufficient". This word, "Was staghnaa", is to think yourself self-sufficient and what does it come from? The word, "Ghanee", which means, "rich" and most of the language that is used in Arabic to describe a person as being boastful or thinking himself important or too important, seeing himself bigger than what he is, they use some form of the word, "rich"; because it is the rich people who always think themselves important and bigger than everybody else. They think their wealth makes them a bigger human being than you. It may make them a bigger force or power than you, but not necessarily a bigger human being than you; because we find the bigger human being among those who are not wealthy. That is the norm that we find. The people who are the bigger human beings are not the wealthy people and the wealthy people are always using their power to get over.

What did the Satan do? In Qur'anic Arabic, "Abaa was stakbara"; not this word exactly, but the same kind of description; he refused. It is from the word, "Kabir, he refused and made himself very big or important". You can see, "Astakbara", is similar to the word, "Astaghnaa", because here is a person who sees himself self-sufficient.

He gave the lie to the goodness

The word, "Kath-thaba", has a shaddah. The word, "lie", in Arabic is without shaddah. It is, "Kathaba." Shaddah means with force, it is more emphatic, it is more pronounced, his problem is more pronounced. The verse says he gave the lie to the goodness. He denied or gave a lie to the goodness.

In Arabic, "Hu", means that his state that G_d is addressing is his spiritual state and G_d will cause this to happen to him through his spirit; not necessarily to his flesh or his intelligence. Maybe he will never become conscious of the punishment that G_d has ordered for him. A lot of people have terrible punishment all of their life and they never see their bad conditions that they are suffering as punishment for their great sins or their wrongs that they are doing. They go on in life.

Problem is in the spirit

Some people go to the hospital for syphilis and then go for gonorrhea and then go for prostate cancer; and then go for triple and quadruple bypass; and then cancer of the tongue or the lip and they never say, "I'm being punished". They just keep trying to pay money to get well and the problem is in their spirit.

Hell fire not for every sinner

You should pay attention to these words, "None shall reach it but those most unfortunate ones" (Qur'an). So hell fire is not for every sinner, is it? It is just for those most unfortunate ones, those who give the lie to the truth and turn their backs. Matters are judged by intentions, so you sin, but you were not doing it with a conscience. You were not aware of the gravity of what you were doing. But then you have another sinner. He's a big sinner. He sees the truth and not only is he sinning doing big sins, but he also sees the truth and turns away from it. So those are the ones in hell fire. If you are not doing it, intentionally, if you don't know any better, what kind of G_d is that Who will burn you up and give you all of that punishment? You don't know any better. You don't see the truth. This is my thinking. I wouldn't have to read this. This is my thinking. It is the thinking I give you. Here it is plain as day.

Heliopolis

You read the description of hell in both the Bible and the Qur'an and if you can understand the language, it's not difficult. It almost can be taken literally…It says hell shall present itself to you and you shall see it with sure vision for certain and that is this time we're living in. The Bible says the people will be going to hell in droves, big crowds, and the Qur'an says this, too, in different ways; almost the same language. The believers will be able to view them from a distance going to hell, but the believers will be going to heaven. How is it going to be that people are going to hell in droves and believers are going to heaven in droves, too and they are going to be distant from each other and be able to view each other? At least the believers will be able to view the disbelievers. That means they are in the same circumstances, only one survived it; the other one didn't. And that is the world right now. Some people are hell bent and you can't turn them around.

New skin is change in cultural excitement

In the Qur'an it says, in hell every time one skin is finished, burned away, right away it will be replaced with another skin. So the torment is continuous, because when a skin is burned it becomes dead. If it is burned enough, the skin itself becomes dead and it doesn't feel. But if you were burned deep you're still hurting, in pain. But now here comes another skin to start the pain up, anew, and fresh, or full of sensitivities, again. So the person experiences the maximum punishment of hell.

Scriptural Reasoning

`Now what is the interpretation? Skin is what you feel with and the Bible from Genesis to Revelations is all about people becoming hardened to conscience, to feelings, where they don't feel anything. They don't feel what they should feel. So replacing the skin means as soon as the people become dead to the punishment, a new sensitivity will be given to them so they can feel it again and go through the same thing, again, over and over.

And that is the way the culture is. It gives those corrupt people one excitement behind another. As soon as one excitement wears off, or becomes dull, not impressing them anymore, they get a new excitement; sensationalism, people living for maximum pleasure, orgiastic nature. They've got to get a high climax. As soon as that one is over they need another charge, another excitement to bring them to a climax. That is their skin being replaced.

The Holy Qur'an is very clear. It doesn't leave you in the dark. But the picture book story of reality is so powerful that you can't show people reality. Their mind is fascinated, fastened to that picture. They think that is real. They think their picture is real. It says in the Qur'an as plain as day, "An naarul haqq, hellfire is reality". It is not myth and superstition. It is reality and it is no new thing. The people of the book they just copied the old ancient oppressors of mankind. The Greeks had a town they called Heliopolis and Helen was the ruler over them too; a wonderful queen. And they gave it her name because under her hell did not even smoke. All the fires were contained so well not even smoke came out.

Idol Worshipers

You have to understand that the world behind paganism, pagan worshipers, was very popular for the Mediterranean and for Europe as well, the Romans, the Greeks, although some of you might not say they are Mediterranean. Spain, Italy, Greece, all those countries in that area, including Egypt, all of them were idol worshipers or pagans. All of the great nations of the past were pagan. Do you think they were stupid enough to really think that those idols were G_d? No. They were no different from our leaders today who see Jesus Christ as an idol but they know that idol is not G_d. So the pagans at that time did likewise. They had their logic. They had their wisdom. They could not manage science and road building, iron works, music and all the things that they developed, they could not have developed all of that and be that stupid.

Idol is a play on idle

We have to get away from this idea of thinking that they worshiped idols and they were savage. No, they had idols and they were as civilized as Manhattan, New York. We may possibly be, today, just as savage and pagan as they were. We are just as savage and pagan, or we are just as much in idol worship as they were in that time. So look at idol worship. What does idol say? It says two things: Idol meaning, bringing to mind something physical, something you can look at and touch. But "idol" is also a play on the word "idle," not busy, wasting your mind, wasting your life. So if you have something occupying your time and it is ruling in your life but it is wasting your intelligence, wasting your human time that G_d gave you to be on this earth to accomplish things, you are worshiping an idol yourself.

"I have to have fun"

I don't care what it is. It could be rap music. It could be a pretty woman, or a pretty boy for you girls. It could be a book that you like that is nothing but past time that is not structuring your life for you. It could be going to movies and just being happy and silly. Your fun can be your worst idol. What do you think of as your fun? Some say, "I have to have my fun." That could be your biggest shirk, your biggest idol. So the logic for saying something is an idol came from wise men who did not believe an object could be G_d. They made idols to represent an image to tell you that if you worship this thing that has attributes of purity it will be good for you. They give you a physical image and then they give you another physical image and they make horns on it or make it look like a demon and they say, "This thing is taboo", or, "It is such and such and it's bad for you." That is the way you talk to a little baby that needs to play with ABC blocks to learn their alphabets. That has lingered around until now.

Don't underestimate those ancient civilizations. That is what I want to tell you. The Qur'an says there were ancient civilizations and many of them had more power than you, speaking of those present ones in the time of Muhammed. And they built skyscrapers taller than yours and look at what was their end. They had more than you and G_d brought them to an end. This is the way the Qur'an addresses those great nations. It did not say they were nothing, stupid. They were mighty but they were not stupid. They were in jahiliyyah. Jahiliyyah doesn't mean just having idols. Jahiliyyah means just what it says, having no sense. They knew how to make money and that was it. They knew how to make money, sex or love. They were good merchants, good poets. Some of them were good family persons, but so narrow in their family love that they would lead their family against your family into tribal wars. That was that.

When the saints go marching in

I am sure the 44th chapter in the Qur'an has reference to the saying in the Bible and of the Christians that 144,000 will be saved because they will be the saints. And 12 times 12 is 144. So 144,000 is universal. That is what it is saying. The righteous are going to be universal, that is what 144,000 says. They're going to be universal. They are not going to be local minded, but global minded; 12:00 p.m. and 12:00 a.m. They are in the 12:00 a.m. because they are the saints. They are working with their brothers and sisters to make the world better. 144,000 will be the saints or the stars. It means the saints, too. There is a song called, *When the Saints Go Marching In*. I used to hear my mother singing that song in the kitchen early in the morning and waking us up from our beds.

7

Mythological Concepts

The Trojan horse was a wooden horse and they put it on wheels so they could roll it or men could pull it. It was all wood, but what is wood? It is a dead tree…The tree bark is like skin on us; for the tree it is a protection for the wood. If all the bark is gone off there is no more protection, so it is dead wood. What does it mean? It means dead culture, culture that can't speak anymore. It has no life of its own anymore and they call it the 5th Column.

Mythological Concepts

 T he Trojan Horse was a wooden horse and they put it on wheels so they could roll it or men could pull it. It was all wood, but what is wood? A dead tree. When wood is like that, stripped, uprooted and stripped of its bark and everything, all the leaves are gone, you're using nothing but the solid mass of it inside.

Greeks bearing gifts

The tree bark is like skin on us; for the tree it is a protection for the wood. If all the bark is gone off there is no more protection. So it is dead wood. What does it mean? It means dead culture, culture that can't speak anymore. It has no life of its own anymore and they call it the 5th Column. So this is saying, "This is the way we're going to penetrate your defenses and get into your society, get into your culture, or your country and defeat you and your people." When they knew anything the horse's door was opened up. It was supposed to be a gift, too. So now what comes out of this gift are people who are going to defeat you. They are coming to take over you and your land; the 5th column. Now the picture is small when you look at it just with your eyes and try to imagine it with your mind without interpretation, but that wood is huge. It is talking about the whole culture of the people.

Entertainment culture takes most people away from G_d

And those five persons, human soldiers, who were in there who came out of there, it might have been a different number but they are not five. They might be 5,000 or 50,000 or 5 million. It is much bigger than what it is saying to us. But the main thing is to see what it is saying. It's saying that, "You're going to be defeated by our plan that we're going to put in your dead culture. We're planning a defeat for you and we'll put it in your dead culture". That is true. Entertainment culture has taken most of our people away from worshiping G_d and trying to make their life better. And that is what it is talking about, entertainment culture, not the general culture.

The Wolf Man

When that woman wrote the story of Frankenstein, the book about the creation of him, she was addressing the same thing that the Trojan horse addresses and it is said in so many ways. Her Frankenstein wasn't enough. They had to bring out a Wolf Man. And here is a man, but when the moon gets full he becomes a wolf. In other words, when his mind tries to perfect itself, he can't do anything but go back to the Roman savage who started their history, they say, from suckling a she wolf. Two boys were nursed by a she wolf and one was killed by the other because he was so stupid his brother killed him. He couldn't make it into the Promised Land.

The style creators

So who is it trying to perfect the mind? It's the religious leadership. They are the ones who want to perfect the mind. They want to perfect the mind. They can't be satisfied with just a human mind. They say, "No, we're more than human. We're human and divine". There he goes back to the savage.

I like fiction and I used to see the Wolf Man change but he would not stay that way. After he stops hearing wolves calling him and the night passes into the day, the wolves are not howling anymore, he comes back to being a normal human being. That is how the style creators who create styles for the public mind regulate us. They darken your intelligence and turn you into a wolf man. Bringing the light back out, cutting the weird sounds off that are coming out of the darkness so that you will not be spooked up, brings you back to intelligent life again. You are wearing a suit and tie going to the bank and doing a good job again. Just the other night you took off your clothes. You had to hurry up and take your shirt off so the animal hair could come all the way out and the animal muscles could swell up, because you were about to ruin your nice shirt and your nice suit. You had to hurry up and get out of it. This is a devilish world, isn't it?

Mythological Concepts

"Take a hike!"

What hurts them more than anything is the birth of Christ Jesus, the birth of Muhammed, peace be upon the prophets, or the birth of a man like me. I hurt them more than anybody. It is more hurting for them because I'm not in a dignified book. I'm not in a world popular book. I don't have any big name and big following. They say, "A little guy like that is destroying our world. He is killing our world in the mind of his people. Go to him and tell him He does not know what he is doing. Take some of our books and let him see what we know." That is what happened, I mean, really. A certain person gave me his books to show me what they know. They said, "Let him see how grand, how massive and how far reaching our knowledge and our thing is. Tell him we said, 'Take a hike'!"

Joseph means increase

I am not doing this to show my knowledge. You gloat over your ability and you do things to show your knowledge. I have no desire to show any knowledge. I do this only to help my people. When I say my people I mean people in my circumstances. If you are white, red, yellow, black, I don't care what color you are. If you have my history of suffering in the darkness of this world and you were not able to get your life up and they were regulating your life with seasons telling you when to live and die, morally, then you are a victim with me and I exist for you.

Al Islam says, yes, Mary was engaged to Yusuf, Joseph, but G_d blessed her with a son and no man touched her. But she was engaged to Joseph. So Jesus Christ says in the Gospel, "He will send you another comforter, the second one will be from Joseph". Joseph means, "increase". So Jesus points to another one, to greater times and great wonders to come, doesn't he? Things will come in abundance, isn't that what was promised. The Qur'an says, "Surely we have given you abundance". How is this great increase realized? The increase is realized because of Joseph. He was given the power to see into matters and he had such powers to see into matters that the crooks didn't even want him around. So they sold him into slavery. "You go to Egypt where they can handle you. We can't handle you". He got there and they liked him so much they put him over the store house and he brought increase to Egypt.

She was not enlightened

Of certain things someone may say, "The reason why Joseph couldn't give birth to him is because Joseph was a man and G_d wanted a son from Himself, not a son from a man of flesh." No, the reason why she couldn't get a son from Joseph is because she was not enlightened. But now a man is coming who is going to be enlightened and when he gets the spirit he is going to get it directly from Joseph. A lot of the so-called scientists or scholars in al-Islam and the religious sciences in al-Islam they know the connection for Muhammed with Joseph and they will use it in their language. "He is another Joseph", they say. We are very close to them. We go right along with their Christian line of reasoning, but G_d has blessed Muhammed with the understanding, so we explain it and they don't."

Possibilities for the ascending human

These are capacities that G_d created the human being with and it comes out and expresses itself in different persons over the long period of time that we are hungering and searching. It comes out in this figure. And I say, "figure", because that is what we have to understand; that this is a progression, designed in human nature and these persons are those who were seen or understood by societies that obeyed, followed them and learned of them as the figure in the living person.

These are possibilities for the ascending human in light, intelligence, the soul, the spirit. These are possibilities for all of us. Allah says there are seven in the heavens and a like number in your selves and there are 114 chapters to the Qur'an. Hundred means you have to first die to your mind that you want to keep and then you can get seven in heaven and seven on earth and it will be complete.

The light at the end

The Christians have three, Father, Son, and Holy Ghost. We have thirty and it means the three have come into the conscious. It is no more spirit, feeling alone. It has dawned in the conscious; thirty chapters, thirty pieces of silver. The secular world, Hollywood, says, you take a silver bullet and fire it into the werewolf to bring him back to his original form. He won't be able to act on his own but at least you can bury him and feel good that he is not a wolf anymore. He's beautiful, he's handsome. His real life comes back to him. He gets it back.

This world is something. That is because of Seth. You see I'm speaking from the wolf man but I'm speaking with the light that G_d has revealed. That is why I can tell you about the wolf being killed with the silver bullet, because Seth has put it also in Hollywood. He hides it all throughout Hollywood, everywhere. That is why the Bible says the light at the end. This is Revelations. This man, John, the Revelator, means he's revealing. The last book of the Bible is talking about the light, how the light will appear and where, first. It appears firstly on the throne and it says the light went out from the throne and filled the whole world, filled the whole earth.

"How can anyone go straight?"

So this is what has to happen to come behind Seth. I'm talking from the Egyptian myth but I'll speak to you from the teaching of Muhammed, the Prophet. What did he say? He said Allah wanted to show Jibril (Gabriel) His world, so He showed Jibril His world and when he saw it he said, "My Lord, how can anyone go astray in such a beautiful world?" Then, Allah, within an instance, caused the world to appear as it would be after Satan decorated it with his enticing things that he was going to put in it, called allurements, fascinations, and the angel, Jibril, saw it and said, "My Lord, how can anyone go straight in such a world?"

"I'm not a man of letters"

In the last book of the Bible is the scene that this is addressing and it didn't just start in Revelations. John, the Revelator, saw it from way back and he brings it forward to show the people, before he passed away. So the reason why light had to appear first on the throne is because the throne was under darkness. What does it mean? The religious seat of power was under darkness so light has to first appear there. And it appeared in Muhammed in the service of G_d; that is the throne. The light comes back to overcome the darkness that was created or put on the world by the Satan, or in the Egyptian myth, by Seth. The Bible speaks of it again when it says darkness prevailed. All over the world there was a famine of hearing the word of G_d. It says not a famine of food. It makes it very clear in the Bible. And in the same connection it says someone came upon a book and took it to a person and said, "Will you read me this?" Obviously, that was an ignorant person, right? That was a person ignorant of the letters of the reading the script. He said will you read this for me?" And the person said, "No, I'm not a man of letters", meaning he was uneducated. He couldn't read literature at all. Then it says the same person continued until he came to another person and he asked him the same question. "Can you read this to me?" And that person said, "I can read, but it is sealed", meaning, "I can read literature. I can read a textbook. I can read the newspaper. But this is not clear reading. This is not reading that you can understand. It's sealed", meaning the true meaning or language is locked up.

And the same book (I'm talking about the Bible) says that a little lamb came up and took the book. Nobody gave it to him; a lamb without spot or blemish. And he took the book and he began reading it and opened up the seven seals.

Judeo-Christian jihad

We are talking about Judeo-Christian Jihad, their struggle to advance their cause. I came to see from studying scripture that much of the ugly language (I say ugly language because that is what it is in the Bible) of their scripture is to deceive the people they feared. And they feared the very people that they had planned on capturing with their Jihad, the pagans. Before Christianity as preached by Peter, Paul and others in their group, their association of preachers or leaders, the pagans believed in idolatry. They were idol worshipers but they were in power. Rome was mighty, very powerful. Just to recall some of the movies you have seen about that life back then is enough for you to understand what exactly my point is and where I'm going with it. They were a savage people, in many ways civilized. But their savagery was so pronounced, so glaring, so present, so big, that it would make a person loving to be right for G_d like me, a loving human being wanting to see human beings in a good human picture, see them almost as animals.

Mythological Concepts

They obviously were not stupid. They made beautiful things. They created beautiful things. They would celebrate and have good times and would be affectionate and loving with one another and they would help and defend one another. But the same people would have for sport the killing of innocent people, their own people as well as slaves they had gotten from other areas of the world they conquered. They would have them trained just like in America, as boxers to go in the ring and box and fight to entertain those who could pay for the admission fee. Their biggest entertainment during the year was to see the gladiators fight each other just like boxers today fight each other for sport. But the purpose was to kill the other, not just to win.

I'm sure you recall movies, television, movie shows, theaters, showing the Romans putting lions on the Christians and having the Christians defenseless in an area like a ring where they couldn't come out of there. In fact, it was worse than the ring, because the officers were standing all around to make sure they would not escape, come out of there. They had to fight lions and so the lions chewed them up. That was their enjoyment, their entertainment.

They enjoyed killing flesh

It was entertainment for the ruler, Caesar, who back then was like the president of the United States. He was the top man in the government sitting there with his chiefs and maybe his wife and daughters, children, enjoying that sport. They loved and enjoyed killing flesh so much that there is a fruit that is named after them. I knew it as a child in Chicago. It is the Indian apple. Some of you might have heard the name of what I'm talking about, the pomegranate. It's also called in the world, Roman apple, or Romaine. That is because when you open it up it looks like it is filled with blood. When you open it up it just bleeds. So they named it that because they saw the Romans as blood-letters, people who liked to spill blood.

Now understand that these people became Catholics. The very people who were persecuting and doing these evils were converted to Christianity. They were no more Roman pagans, they were Roman Christians. And I have visited the Vatican and seen their chief. He is not Caesar, he's the Pope (John Paul II) and a beautiful, loving man that I embraced who was working hard for justice around the world; for justice to come to the suffering people of the world and to have love come into the hearts of leaders of the world for the people they are ruling over. This was a wonderful man. He was not like those Caesars who were enjoying spilling the blood of innocent people, senseless enjoyment and senseless destruction of human life. This is a big change that has come about and we must give Christianity the credit.

They were converted to a much better world and great suffering has been done away with, although we know even the wolf man, he is beautiful most of the time. But when the full moon comes he turns into a bad creature. So we will see times when they were tested by wars, etc. and they became very brutal, again. However, that was the army. It was a selected group for them fighting for their country and doing horrible, brutal things in the world, great conquerors, and still great fighters. Greece also was converted from paganism to Christianity so all these great nations that we see associated with the West they were converted to Christianity from pagan life and we may give Christianity the credit. But the ones who planned that were not Christians, they were Jews.

Frankenstein

The Qur'an says they didn't kill him. They didn't crucify him. But the word in the Qur'an for crucify means leave him for his body to stiffen, Riga mortis to set in. And they know all of this. Hollywood, they made Frankenstein and Frankenstein was formed of dead bodies. He was not taken from the living but taken from the dead. He was formed of dead bodies and then the parts of the dead bodies were put together to complete his body and to present him in the form of a man in every respect. Then he was put on a slab and raised up high in the sky during a storm so the lightening would strike him, directly and bolts were put in his neck to take the electricity coming into his dead body.

Bolts were there and his body was brought to life by the lightening. But when they brought him down and took him off of the slab he still remembered the position he was supposed to have (arms outstretched and stiff). This is the position he had in the sky. So now he's walking down here and if he wants to speed up a little bit the old groove (arms outstretched and stiff) takes over because he wants to speed. He's not thinking too carefully. So Hollywood has given us a meaning of the cross. You have been fed a lot of dead knowledge from the world that died and you have been given jolts of electricity. You go and listen to a sermon and you get jolts of electricity or power and you'll be quiet and almost about to go to sleep and the preacher says something that jolts you. "Yes, thank you Lord! Thank you Jesus!"

You go out of church and all you can do when you have to speed up is form a cross. You can't go anywhere. Your life is checked. You can't get out of the position they put you in, fixed. And the preacher is not satisfied until he has your mind fixated. When he thinks he really has you locked up by what he's giving you then he's ready to give you direction. He's ready to tell you, "Put something in the offering". But he's not going to give you instructions until he knows you have become fixated, and he jolts you into a cross.

The woman who wrote the book (Mary Shelley) obviously had insight into scripture and she saw the average convert as Frankenstein. But look, frank means open. Frankenstein, that is Jewish, there is no doubt about it. Frankenstein is a Jewish name. So she is saying the Jews crucified the Christians. We know they didn't crucify Jesus Christ, so there is nobody left but his followers who were ignorant. And it turns out he was a good guy, because they made a Frankenstein to show he really was a psychotic criminal. He had a good nature and in that movie a girl lost her balloon. It escaped her and he got it and took it back to the girl. The little girl was afraid of him but after he showed that kindness to her she wasn't afraid of him. And then they showed him with a wife, too, and she was screwed up more than he was. She was really out of it.

The Number of the Beast

Nothing that has been prophesied is let out of what is going on right now in this world. Everything is happening right now. When I was reading the Bible I came across 666. And I had heard about it as a young child in the Temple listening to the my father and his ministers preach. I heard about 666 as the number of the beast, in Revelations it appears. "He who has wisdom let him count the number of the beast, for it is the number of a man and his number is six threescore and six". That is how it is given. I have always been a student in my mental makeup so I didn't just read like the other ministers did. I wanted to know why three score is another six. So I looked in the dictionary and I found three score is twenty so three times twenty is sixty. So that is six plus sixty that will be sixty-six, right? I'm trying to bring you along. I know what I'm saying. I just want to make sure you know.

So that will be six hundred and sixty six. That is in Revelations. What I was giving in the Temple was what I found in the Bible when I read it and that was that the weight of tax collectors was six, six, six. So it is not only associating this number of the beast is not only associated with a wicked man or a wicked figure of a man who is Shaitan also the figure of Shaitan or the image of Shaitan, the Satan, the devil but it is also give as the number of taxes that was collected in one collection during the time period when a certain king for the Jews was not popular with the Jews. He was very unpopular with the Jews. This king was being criticized to them by Jews for taxing them too heavily.

Fight the schemes of Satan

Then *Revelations* comes much later in the Bible and identifies this number with a beast and a man who is beastly, or a beast, and we know that figure as Satan or the devil. There is in the reported sayings of the Prophet Muhammed, the Dajjal. He is pictured in hadith riding a donkey and he's supposed to be one-eyed. One of his eyes is blind; one he doesn't see with. That symbolizes or says by way of symbolism he had no moral vision at all. He was not moral at all. He was completely, totally immoral, blind to moral concerns. He's pushing materialism. Don't look for a person. Don't even look for a race. But look for conditions. The Prophet told us to fight conditions, not to look for a devil in form. He told us that when G_d revealed Qur'an to him and he reported it to the following and then educated, taught them on that particular concern where G_d says, "Fight the schemes of Satan for his schemes are weak."

Khamar is anything that takes away your clear mind

We understand, G_d makes it very plain in Qur'an, not taking anything for drinking is Khamar. But understand it does not mean whiskey or wine, something with alcohol in it. It has no direct reference to alcohol at all. Its reference is to anything that takes away your clear mind and makes you intoxicated; anything that intoxicates you and interferes with your ability to see clearly, behave clearly and have moral control of your thinking and behavior. Intoxication, that is what it is against. It is against any form of intoxication. If somebody says, "Reefers is not in the Qur'an. The Qur'an doesn't condemn reefers." If it interferes with your mind, clear thinking, if reefers make you high, then it is intoxicating and you become intoxicated. So it's a drug that intoxicates, so it is forbidden. Anything like that is forbidden. You can apply this to, also, an indecent invitation from a man to a woman or from a woman to a man. A poet speaks of love being a wine and when you look at the word Khamr, khamar, khamr is intoxication and khemar is hijab. Women used to wear, like they still do, a big covering over their head that comes out over the shoulders and this covering is called a shawl that women wear. And you see these women from Saudi Arabia, the Emirates and different places now. They are in magazines, in the news and on TV, in the market places and you'll see them with the big head piece on. It is so big it goes over the shoulders and it covers part of the upper part of the body. They wear them nicely. It looks stylish. They look real nice. That is a khemar and the reason why it is called khemar is because the root is to intoxicate.

Isis is spiritual sciences

It was never meant for us to think that the moon in our esoteric, secret language that came from Mr. Fard, is the physical moon that you saw last night, tonight, or see in the daytime if it appears. It is not that moon at all. What is the moon? It is the moon in ancient Egyptian myth. It is Isis. She was the moon and she eclipsed her father, the sun. His name in myth is Osiris. She found a way to eclipse him and eclipse up there means one thing in astronomy. But eclipse in government means one rule overpowered the other and a new rule came into place. This is the way we understand Isis and Osiris.

Isis represents the ancient high science called, spiritual sciences, that has been embodied in deep psychology. Isis represents that body of knowledge. She is a human personification of that knowledge. So they are not talking about two humans and they certainly are not talking about the moon and the sun up there in the heavens.

Thoughts for Searchers

Osiris is the social sciences

They are talking about a knowledge that takes care of their society like the sun takes care of earth. It warms it up. It gives it guidance. It opens darkness so life can see how to move about and it grows your food. It grows things so that you can have more production. It drives the clouds with the wind and it sends you rain. It sends you darkness, the fire the sun, the heat that is associated with the sun. Heat is not associated with the moon. It is associated with the sun. That is high science in the social side of life, the social community, the social sciences, Osiris. Isis is the spiritual sciences that I said also embodied psychology. Psychology started with the spiritual sciences.

Spiritual sciences eclipsed the social sciences

When the spiritual sciences are made so attractive and interrupt the flow of the social sciences and the spiritual sciences become very attractive, so attractive that the social sciences are not in focus anymore like it be used to be (not in the conscious), the spiritual sciences have now eclipsed the social sciences. Isis is the moon and Osiris is the sun.

Hemlock: Blood Lock

Galileo, the scientist, look how he came and just tried to give true sciences to that particular order of his day. And what did they do with him because he was saying things that disproved the way they were perceiving the earth (i.e., as a table, flat)? He said, "No, it is not flat. It is round." He was trying to connect them with the universe, how the earth is just a body among the other bodies. But they didn't want that, because they said, "This is the center of the universe because G_d's man is here. G_d's word is here so this is the center of the universe." When he came and gave them the truth of astronomy what did they do to him? They arrested him. They arrested Socrates and they gave him hemlock, a poison for him to take and got rid of him.

In the word hemlock, "hem" means blood. Lock means, "lock up the social life. Don't let the social life out". I'm telling you exactly what happened. He was not just a man being killed. He was a freedom being killed. "Let's stop this social freedom. Let's stop this movement of social sciences. Let's kill it, lock it up, stop it."

So that is what they did. In arresting Galileo for going against their perception of the universe or perception of the earth they were establishing him as a sign that we are not going to have this, you coming up with these sciences. If you lock the blood what do you have? You have Riga mortis, or blood ceasing to flow. So do you see the cross, again? There's the crucifixion. They crucified him for what? They crucified him for bringing the truth of the sciences into the world and they crucified Jesus, the same, for what? They crucified Jesus Christ for bringing the truth and the sciences into the world.

Same world crucified Galileo and Jesus Christ

So don't separate what happened to Galileo from what happened to Jesus Christ. Don't separate them. It is the same world doing the same thing; afraid of the truth getting out that will shake their kingdom, cause their kingdom to fall. History tells us that the Church for all that time after Jesus Christ, except for rare changes, when you had a good man come in, he wouldn't last. They would soon get rid of him. The order was an order that oppressed the masses or their public and also oppressed the women, females.

Greedy for the material world

The Bible and the story of what happened are saying quietly that this new order after Jesus Christ has material greed. They were greedy for the material world. The world that they condemned and said, "No, you cannot ascend up to G_d unless you first divorce yourself from this world", they were greedy for it and eating it up; ruling the people above their heads, up in the sky. And at the same time, as the Nation of Islam teacher said, they put us in the sky, the feet represents us, the spiritual life. The feet represent us politically, too. No government can establish itself in strength unless it establishes itself upon the masses of the people. The masses of people are the feet of the establishment, whether you look at it politically, or you look at it, spiritually.

Thoughts for Searchers

Bible shows truth and the opposition to it

The Bible condemns it, too. See how the Bible is a book that shows the truth and then shows the opposition to the truth; shows what is going to happen, because of the opposition and shows what's going to be victorious over the opposition. This is the Bible. It has all this in it. You can't say it is not a divine book. It just gives you the world, the corruption, with the light and shows you how the light is in conflict with the corruption and how the light, eventually at the end, wins. It is victorious.

8

Spirit and Spirituality

Birds have always been as a symbol of the soul or the spirit in the human soul...In ancient times and even now they believed that when you sleep the spirit in the form of a bird leaves your body and returns to your body at the time of awakening... The ancients believed that when we go to sleep that one bird separates, leaves us, and one stays, because your conscious is your world and your subconscious, or part of your subconscious, belongs to G_d.

Thoughts for Searchers

Birds have always been as a symbol of the soul or the spirit in the human soul...In ancient times and even now they believed that when you sleep the spirit in the form of a bird leaves your body and returns to your body at the time of awakening, for you getting up out of your sleep. And some believe, like in the Qur'an, that there are two birds inside you and one bird leaves and the other bird stays with you to guard you and be with you during your sleep. But one bird goes away. The bird that stays with you is the bird of your conscious that knows your life. It is your conscious but is symbolized as a bird. It stays with you and appears in the form of dreams or whatever. It comes up in your dreams, but it stays with you.

The ascendant spirit

And the other bird takes off and goes away. That is the bird, the spirit, that G_d created to connect with Him; the ascendant spirit; but not necessarily ascending, because if your mind is not for ascension, the bird does not go anywhere except where you are. It stays right in the realm of your reality. Though it left your body, it is still in the realm of your reality. It did not go up in the heavens. It is still down here, but it is separated from your body. This is a belief and I believe it is true. These ancient people who came up with these ideas and they fixed them in myth, culture, and history. They had experience over a long period of time and most likely when we discover something we will find that there were people who discovered it before us and they left it in symbols.

The real path to G_d

The ancients believed that when we go to sleep that one bird separates, leaves us, and one stays, because your conscious is your world and your subconscious, or part of your subconscious, belongs to G_d. It is His Sanctuary and He says He would not allow anyone to plow in His Sanctuary. So when the brain is not ruling us, that bird flies away until we wake up again; then it comes back. It stays with us until we wake up to it. If we never wake up to it we die having never found the real way to G_d, the real path to G_d.

Spirit and Spirituality

The eve and the morning were the first day

The wife of Adam, peace be on him and her, too, she is never given a name in Qur'an. The Arabs have a name for her in tradition, but in Qur'an you do not find her name. You only find where Allah says He made from one nafs, one soul, a mate and they became mates, male and female and they produced many men and women. He is from the soul. He is not flesh. At that time, he is not being addressed as a flesh body. When it says, "Nafsin wahidah," he is being addressed as a spiritual body.

He made them from one soul. Nafs means person but in this respect is never thought of as a physical or material person or as flesh. The flesh body is called something else; like in English we say person, body. We have different terms. When you say, body, you think of a material body. When you say person you think of a particular person by name. When you speak of persons as persons you speak of them with some knowledge of them as a person. And if you have knowledge of them as a person, your knowledge of them as a person is more important than your knowledge of them as flesh.

I can see a person one time and see what you've been seeing for fifty years and I don't need to see any more. I saw his flesh enough. For just a couple of minutes that was enough. I don't have to see his flesh for fifty years. But you have seen what I have not seen if I am just meeting that person. You have seen the person inside of the flesh and that is what this is talking about.

Your true self is your soul

From the same word, nafs, you get psyche, psychology. This word, nafs, in Qur'an and the Arabic language is more closely related in meaning to the psyche of the human person than it is to anything else. And from psyche you get psychology. Each one of us has our personal psychology. For each person there is a psychology; not only a psyche but there is also a psychology. Psychology means the way you are most likely to respond and behave spiritually. That is why I said you are a spiritual body more so than a material body. In the world we study it and call it psychology. In religion we call it spiritual sciences, the spiritual sciences of the human nature and behavior. So from, "Nafsen wahedah (one soul)", He made two. We have to get away from thinking of Adam and Eve in the material sense, flesh...You are not your body. You are not flesh. More importantly, you are the person in the flesh and that is spiritual. So your true self is your soul.

The son of man

When the mate is called Eve it is the beginning of darkness. The sun is going down so this is in line with the meanings in scripture. The one I'm referring to right now is the Bible, Old and New Testament. At the end of the Bible the man is called "Sun." He is called, "Son of man." Jesus said, "Who do you say I, the son of man, am?" This is Jesus Christ's question to his disciples. He questioned them. He wanted them to tell him how they perceived him, how they understood him. So he said to them, "Who do you say I, the son of man, am. Who am I?" That is what he asked. And he said, "The son of man".

He said to them in words, "Now, let us begin from this reality, that I am the son of a man". Someone may say, "Oh no, he is not the son of man, He is the son of Mary." You are correct and I am correct. He is the son of Mary and he is also the son of man. How come he is the son of man? Because that is what the Bible says. The genealogy of Jesus Christ is traced back to Adam, a man and it says tracing the genealogy back to men they knew in history and it mentioned Adam and it says, "Who was created by G_d."

Jesus Christ is the son of Adam, isn't he? Is it any different in Al Islam? Muhammed showed us the Ascension (Miraj) and he said to Jesus Christ and John, "Peace be on you Brother Jesus and Brother John." Isn't that what he said? And then he went on up into the Ascension. But first he greeted Adam and he said, "Father". And then he greeted Jesus Christ and John. He said, "Brother". So if they are his brothers aren't they the sons of Adam, too? And when he went to the top he greeted Abraham and he said to him, too, "father". He said, "Peace to you Father Abraham". He didn't say, "Brother". So they are brothers, all of the men are brothers and there are only two fathers, Adam and Abraham, peace be on all of them. I am trying to show you that both religions are saying the same thing. One comes to give more light and understanding.

Spirit and Spirituality

Spirit is the whole life

The Bible says the life began with Eve and the evening and the morning was the first day. This is a different life of physical people. Religion, the scripture, is not about the life of biology. It is not to teach us biology. It is not on biology, it is on spirituality. It is on the spiritual side that is the life. The spiritual is the whole life. It is the true life. It is the real life.

Man did not have life until what happened? G_d breathed into him of His Spirit and he became a living being, a living soul. He did not have life until the spirit went into him. Then he was a living soul. This growth is in two dimensions. One is the physical dimension and when you study the human life in the physical dimension you are studying biology or some kind of science of the physical life. That is not the Qur'an. That is not the Bible. That is not religion. When you study people as spiritual beings that emotional side is another side, isn't it? It is part of our spirituality. The emotions are a part of our spirituality.

Woman is spirituality, man is spirit

I don't say all these words are perfect because they are not perfect for me, i.e, calling a woman, Eve. To me, spirituality is not perfect for understanding. But when you look at scripture to see woman's nature, to see what type of nature she represents, Eve, the first woman, refers to the spiritual life, the spiritual side; but not spirit with direction. This is spirituality.

The woman is spirituality, the man is spirit. One is the context, the other one is the movement, the drive in the context. Why is man like that? It is like that because G_d made man, the male, to be the provider; as Allah says in Qur'an, He made man to be the provider. In earlier life when society had not formed all of this public life that we have to support our personal life and our home life, the man was responsible for the family, for his household, or if he got with his neighbors it was a tribal thing, it was still family. They went out to hunt and bring back food.

Going out to hunt educated the man in the world. The man became educated in the world and the woman was left back. She was not educated in the world, so what happened to her? She became more spiritual than her men who were on the outside. Even today, who do you find most in the Church? The woman. And it looks like the mosque is turning out to be that way, too. The longer I preach the more I see females growing in the mosque and males, their numbers are dwindling. The female numbers are increasing. Women are more in touch with human life. They have to take the babies from infancy, from the womb and they have to care for those babies until they are ready to go out with the men into the public life. The woman is more spiritual so she is figured as spirituality and the man is figured as spirit.

Adam was a land man

The arrow that is used as the sign for the man, it is something that is designed to go fast and far in the wind. The woman's sign is that of the cross. Imagine all lines being equal, all angles being equal that is the female sign. What does it mean? It means to check, control, keep in certain boundaries. And isn't that the responsibility of the female, the mother, at home, to keep her children in check; to keep them at home in the private life and not let them go out and be influenced by the world? So the signs are right.

The Qur'an says, "Allah taught Adam the names of all of the things" and He made Adam from the dust of the earth. Adam was a land man and he became an industrialist and the industrialists give us these signs. He knows better. He is Adam, we don't know. G_d taught Adam all the names; not us. But He reveals to whomsoever he pleases what He wants to reveal. To whom He reveals there is nothing to cause him to stray. To whom He gives guidance there is nothing to cause him to stray. And from whom He withholds guidance there is nothing to guide him. This is Allah in the Qur'an. You have to speak for the male. It comes out of the circle. The arrow should be coming out of the right side. If that is a face looking at us then the arrow should be on its left side. The male comes out of the female and I've never known one to come here any other way.

Soul and spirituality first

Eve and the morning is the first day, so spirituality is first. Soul and spirituality come before consciousness in the world. Then man gets an interest as a hunter or as an explorer, as a curious person out in the world. He begins to get many interests and those interests have homes. They are based back home. They start back home. I have a wife to take care of. I have a wife and children and I need to take care of them. I have to go find supplies and bring them home, find the needs for the wife and children and bring them home. So his life is worldly drawn, worldly directed. It is drawn by the world. It draws him out there and her life is in check.

This is the first meaning for Adam and Eve, human spirituality, and the aim in that spiritual nature or in that body we call the spiritual life, or the spirituality, is to go from private life or from home life and engage the whole environment. That is what the male has done. He's come from the private life and gone out. Why does he want to take this life out to the public or out in the world? He was forced to go out in the world himself to provide sustenance for his family. He goes back home to his wife so he can find comfort, tranquility, in her, to find peace there in her, because he is of her and she is of him. So he goes back home from his weary day in the world hunting and whatever he had to run up against. It was tiring and not peaceful all of the time for him so he goes back home to his people. Then he has to go back out again to the world.

Nature will urge him

So he came from her. They came from one another, each other, and there they find their peace at home with each other. But now he is forced to go out in the world to provide the material needs for the home and other needs come into play, too. He is providing the material needs for her and it is very difficult going from a world that's dead to the life that he really identifies with and his wife and family identifies with. Therefore, it is a trying thing just to keep going out. Eventually, nature will urge him, saying, "Convert these people out here to your life so you will have peace out here in the world, also." That is the motivation. The motivation, eventually, is that I have to do something about these people. They don't have the life we have and it is hell coming out here every day to earn a living and going back home.

Thoughts for Searchers

Conclusion of all things prophesied in the scriptures

When he starts out he soon finds out it is a hard job. He cries to G_d and in time G_d answers and then there is a messenger, a prophet, from G_d preaching to the world. But all of this starts from Adam. We shouldn't leave that reality. This all started with Adam and he was made from dust, clay, from the ground. The Bible doesn't say dust. It says from the ground and Allah (in Qur'an) says also from the ground, in Arabic, "Ard" and it means, "The earth or ground".

So let's not leave the idea that we have been conditioned to separate these two movements; the movement of man as a builder, an industrial person, and the movement of man as a soul needing peace and satisfaction in order to be comfortable in the soul, not in the flesh. We separate these two and we come now to the conclusion of these things. That is where we are right now in the world, at the conclusion of all these things prophesied in the scriptures.

An industrious man

We look at the religious world and we don't see as much evidence of knowledge and meaning as we see in the world of the industrialists. The world of the industrialists includes all of the scientists. Industry is not just brick making or stone cutting. Industry is also agriculture and all the other sciences you can think of are all tied to industry. He taught Adam the names of all the things. When the industrialist comes in he builds the buildings, the physical facility, to accommodate whoever it is. Then, when that facility is up you will see the doctor rent an office. You will see everybody coming to rent spaces that were made available by the industrialist, by the builder. But the industrialist is also a banker, isn't he? When you say industry generally speaking you are referring to everything that is done to provide for human needs in their environment.

All of the medical sciences, everything, is part of the industry. But now we have come to see industry focus only on factory machinery. To us that is the meaning of industry, but industry is also the husband who cares about being gainfully employed so he can provide for his family. You would call him an industrious man, wouldn't you? Industry covers everything, all production that serves human needs and that is Adam. Man was created for that purpose, to be a provider or a maintainer as the Qur'an says.

I see more evidence in the industrial world that they have more knowledge in the meaning of the scriptures than the Church and all of these other religious places, religious establishments have. They have very little understanding. That is why Adam has become the head of the Church. In these United States who is the head the Church? They are separated aren't they? They did not say separate but equal, did they? They said the separation of church and state. They did not say the separation in equality of church and state.

The boss is the mayor. The boss is the man in this society we live in, the United States of America. Stick with scripture. Do not leave where I am. The boss is the man and the woman is his helper, helpmate, helpmeet, whatever you want to call it; that is, in this world and it is for true life. In the Bible it says the head of the woman is the man. I am giving you the exact words. And the head of the man is G_d. This is the Bible.

Spirit means having a direction

So how do these meanings progress? The meanings progress or originate from that perception that woman is typical of human spirituality. Do you see how I am saying that? I say typical because there is an exception to every rule. Man is typical of human spirit. Spirit means going out and having a direction like an arrow or a spear. They call it spirit. A spear is a rod or a stick with an arrow head on it and it is made like that to travel fast and a long distance in the air.

Now the meanings have progressed, so you have now not one Mary. You have Jesus Christ one man, but you do not have one Mary, do you? There are four Mary's in the Bible; Mary the mother of Jesus Christ, upon her be peace and three others. All of these Mary's are not having the same meaning. The meaning of Mary, the mother of Jesus Christ, is not the same as those other three Mary's. They are different.

Thoughts for Searchers

"Why have you crucified me continuously?"

There's only one Jesus Christ, but in the Bible he said, "Why have you crucified me continuously?" So that means they have crucified him in others; not just him in his own person, but also others they have crucified. They say they crucified Saint Peter. Again, Jesus says, "As you have done to the least of these you have done onto me." How are we to understand that? It is not talking about a Jew or an African. He is talking about a spiritual body that is in all people, that is in every man. That is why he said, "I in you and you in me," speaking to his followers.

Christ inside the nature

All of these are not the same, because if we understand it John was also; though he was John by mission and by his role he was John, Yahya. John in the Bible, wasn't he also Christ Jesus inside his nature? He had Christ inside his nature. We have to get away from seeing these figures as flesh, or members of a race and see them in the real meaning that we find in scripture. You should see them as spiritual types inside of the human body or the human nature. They are types inside of the soul of human beings.

Woman is man also

Then, can't you understand if I say to you, "Woman is also man?" That is given in the story, the myth, mystical story of the mother of Jesus Christ, peace be upon them; that G_d made a man from a woman, not from a man. No matter how we translate it or interpret it, if G_d made a man from a woman and no man is his father then there must have been man in woman; but not the flesh and blood man you are thinking about; the real type. The drive (man) to go out and make the world fit for human life is also in woman and the proof of it is that she gave birth to the spirit without a man touching her.

From dust to industry

I heard one imam of the immigrant Muslims, those who came here from overseas who have been here a long time say, "Allah made a man from the ground without mother or father; that was Adam. Then He made a man from a woman without a father and that is Christ." That stuck in my mind and I said to myself, "G_d was obligated to do that, if He says He made man from the ground, the material reality, and we see we come from mother, male and female.

So if G_d said He made man from the ground due respect to the woman says He has to make man from a woman. We know we do not see any men made from the ground. We see all men coming from women like every other human being comes from a woman. So to give respect to woman the reality of how our history is just that man is establishing his life. I'm speaking in the plural not just one individual. He established the life for himself and others. He established that life, firstly, and the history of the progress for human society is addressing, directly, the abundant resources in the ground. That is why I use the expression, "From dust to industry". He starts first in the ground. That is scripture and that is reality.

Man's work has given us man's world

After a while the public life becomes such a big life with comforts and everything built into it that it becomes a life separate from the material efforts of man. It becomes education, schools, churches, religious places of worship, and cultural places. It becomes government, political owners, all of these developments. Now we have a new reality and it is not the original ground that man survived upon. This man's work has brought in another world.

A new man-made order

Man's work has given us man's world. For want of a better expression I say, "Man's world". It is not the ground producing the thinking, the human sensitivities, the spirit and all that makes my soul or my life. It is not the ground anymore feeding that directly, but it is a new order, a new man-made order that is feeding that. So the ground is not producing us directly anymore. It is the city life or the community life that is producing us. We're getting our new minds and our new leaders, our new careers, our new occupations and whatever we are getting all from this new reality. It has now become the mother. It is the mother, now, not Mother Earth. It is society that is giving birth to us.

So we should see that the real progress for industrious man is coming from agricultural life, the simple life of the farm or something, to the life of city builders. If you notice in scripture, especially the Bible, that it is the big cities, the big populations, that are given all female names. Nineveh, Babylon, all of these cities are called women in the Bible, because those circumstances are now producing people, producing their thinking and interests.

Look at how the woman changes from spirituality. Her perception, firstly, is spirituality. Now she is a big mama. She's accommodating all of these things. So to say that woman is spirituality is not enough. Woman is spirituality. Woman is environment. The environment produces us, but the environment changes. With man's progress the environment changes. The environment becomes more complex and much more productive, in time. Get the sex thing out of the study of knowledge and religion. It is not about sex as we understand sex.

Look at how the Bible starts off with Eve, why? Because those men back there at that time, when they were writing scripture or scripture was being inspired and conceived, those men were bothered already by big populations that were giving themselves to sin and corruption. So the allusion here to Eve is that we begin in ignorance; not only that, we begin in spirituality. There was no light. There was darkness and in time born of and out of the darkness comes the light and the light is the sun. Light is symbolized as the sun.

Jesus: The sunlight of man

So when Jesus Christ asked, "Who do you say I the son of man am", he was speaking of himself in the same sense as scripture before him spoke of man; man both as a flesh and blood person but also as enlightenment, the sun of man; the enlightenment for man but also of man. Man's enlightenment came out of man. Knowledge is in the head of somebody and they share it with us. Knowledge is light then it comes to us out of the head of somebody. So the son (sun) of man is the one who gives light to mankind or becomes the light for mankind. The one who comes to light for mankind, Jesus Christ, was alluding to that, "Who do you say I the son of man am?"

Spirit and Spirituality

So son is an allusion on or to the light of man, or the enlightenment of man. Then we should think of Adam, too, as an illumined body, not just as a body or a spirit inspired and made conscious, knowledgeable, and wise by G_d. He represents a body of light and this kind of reasoning is not just limited to people of the Book. It is all around the world, all the myths in the world have started just like that.

"My mother is black"

I was studying about Buddha in Buddhism and he says of himself, "My mother is black". This is Buddha talking in that religious, spiritual language. He pursued his destiny or his calling and something was driving him to search the darkness. His mother was black and he was driven or motivated to search the darkness. So that mother is not a biological flesh and blood mother. He is talking about his mother as his country, his environment that he was born in that was in ignorance. He saw it in ignorance like Muhammed, the Prophet, saw the Arabs of the land where he was born in ignorance, darkness. Buddha saw his people, the way they were living in darkness and he says, "My mother is black". He goes on to the road of enlightenment and as he progresses in that road he comes to see the nature of his society as his mother.

Adam was the first light for man

So the first mother he saw was the land that gave birth to him, or the land that supported him. That was his first mother, the society that he was member of. Then later he sees the nature, he gets wisdom and insight and he sees the nature explaining their behavior. When you see nature you see what explains how what manifests, the how is shown, the outer picture. Nature is referring to the inside, the inner picture, the necessary workings of things within a body that give it character or give it design. That is nature. So he finally gets insight into the nature of his society and he is still seeing his mother as black.

Absence of education first darkness

The first black is the darkness that is the absence of education or absence of knowledge. Darkness that is the absence of education or absence of knowledge is the first darkness. The next darkness is the nature itself, those things that operate to make things what they are and to make them perform as they performed and his mother is black. He says he finally was illuminated. He reached illumination and he became a body of light. That meant G_d. I know they don't say G_d in Buddhism, but I'm saying G_d. I believe in G_d. He illumined him, made him see and understand things and he became the light for his society. The illumined one they called him, shining bright with light. Is that any different from Adam? No, it is the same subject. Here is Adam, the man of the ground, man working the earth. G_d blessed him to see inside things and know the nature of things and give them their names. So actually he was an illuminated body, too, wasn't he? Yes. He was the first light for man, father for mankind.

The Spiritual Ascension of Man

The sky is the level above us. It is part of the earth, too, if you understand it. But it is a level high above ground in a region above ground called the skies. It refers to the spiritual side, the spiritual life, but not spiritual life seen as emotional life. No, it refers to spiritual life seen as the need to ascend in intelligence and understanding. So the sky represents the need inside of us to ascend, to graduate, one level to another and keep going higher and higher in our spirituality for the purpose of rational, clear understanding. So it is the ascent of man. Sky represents the ascent of man and Allah says in Qur'an that there are seven tracts above you, or seven orbits above you and seven within yourselves.

Inherent urge in human nature

Now these are firmaments. The Bible calls them seven firmaments and the translator of the Qur'an some of them also use the same term as the Bible, firmaments. What do you have in the term firmament? You have firm foundations in the sky and seven within us. So the meaning of seven within us down here on earth means that this is a property of human life and nature. Whatever is in the sky it is a property or they are properties of human life and nature. The potential is in us. The capacity and potential to rise in our nature to that height of spirituality and intelligence is in all of us. It is in all people.

Spirit and Spirituality

So when the Qur'an says likewise in us down here on earth, in the people down here, it means that we have an inherent ability to rise up to those levels where Abraham was in the highest level until Muhammed and he ascended to Abraham's level, but he didn't just ascend. He also traveled in the sky to the farthest mosque and all that has meaning. It is in Jerusalem, meaning that G_d revealed to Muhammed the ascent of man's nature, man's intelligence, his spirituality and his intelligence. And G_d also connected him with the symbol, or with the inherent urge in human nature to do better and achieve more, symbolized in the Ka'bah. It is a sign of that potential in all of us. The Ka'bah is a sign of that.

Destiny of man a purpose to be reached

And Muhammed was lifted up from there to the highest level on which Abraham is given, the seventh level, the highest heaven. Then he was caused to travel from that place to Jerusalem that represented for the people of scripture their great community achievements. They say there was no success, or achievement, for the people, the Jews, like that of Solomon where they had a government that welcomed all people; and the highest wisdom and the greatest industry or productivity, they realized it under Solomon. He is also called Solomon, the Great.

G_d connected Muhammed with that. So we're talking about human potential, human capacity to ascend, to grow, to produce more and become more productive; what is naturally in us. So it is talking about heredity, what is inherent. This ascending and expanding of our nature to take in more and produce or give out more, this is G_d's purpose for every human being and therefore it is the divine destiny. So we think of destiny and divine destiny as a place. No, it is not a place. It is a purpose to be reached.

The inherent life

In the scripture and in the Qur'an it mentions twelve springs in connection with the leadership of Moses. It refers to what is universal, what is true for human life everywhere. Why is it twelve and not twenty four? It is twelve because twenty four is the subconscious, or the night. Now we know it is not exactly twenty four, but certain times in the year the nights are the same length as the day and then it changes. Night becomes shorter, day becomes longer, but these twelve have always been signs or symbolic code words that hint their reference to what the subject is all about.

This subject is all about the inherent life. It is the inherent life and twelve says it is universal, the same for all people; the same for the whole world. The world is twelve, referring to a conscious world and the world is twelve, again, referring to an unconscious world, or a world not published, a secret world. Some say twelve springs mean the twelve tribes, but the deeper meaning that is the more valued meaning is to understand that these are spiritual urges in

Twelve springs of purity

When it says springs gushing up from the earth that is an urge, a force and it is pushing up through the earth and pushing up purifies it. You send water up through sand and rocks and they serve as a purifier or a filter cleansing the water. So these are healthy springs not springs of corruption like some think. If G_d revealed twelve springs to Moses or to the people of Moses then you should understand that these twelve springs are twelve springs of purity, or twelve springs of moral purity. It is an urge in the nature to take the human life to where G_d wants it to go. G_d doesn't want it to remain dormant resting under the earth out of the sight of society. He wants it to spring up and show itself to the world and give its purity and its light to the world. This water, whether it comes from the sky or under the earth, is water that feeds all life. No life can begin without water. So twelve springs refers to the inherent urge which is in the spiritual body or in human spirituality to rise up and serve the purpose given to it by its Creator and that is to feed life and support life's form.

Fishermen of men

When Jesus went looking for the people or the persons who would help him with his mission he was forming a group of leaders to work with him for the mission. He went to get fishermen because they were skilled in getting intelligent life out of the water. Fish are intelligent and they represent intelligent life of the water. He wasn't satisfied with them just being professionals on the water bank. He said, "Come and follow me and I will show you how to become fishermen of men." So they left the water and went inland, not to fish for spiritual intelligence, but to become those who could bring out of the material world life for building the new world of Jesus Christ, the new kingdom, or the kingdom to come.

But look at who he picked. He didn't go fishing on the land, first. He went to the water and then he brought those who knew-the professionals of the water. He brought them to land and then he trained them in how to become professionals on the land. It is beautiful and that is the way it should be. So if you don't have such followers or such persons representing that science that is universal, twelve, that stands up anywhere and everywhere on the planet earth; if you don't have such men trained in that, you have to produce such men trained in that. You have to produce those leaders

Spirituality can be rested down and up

I don't think he was necessarily saying that those 12 persons were qualified in the sciences. They were fishing and they were able to fish and bring them out, but just religious psychology can do that. The proof is that these churches convert people to their way or to their knowledge, their order, or their religion, but I doubt if they know what we're talking about here. But they have a natural ability to appeal to man's waters or to human spirituality. They have a natural ability to do that. I understand that this spirituality is rested spirituality, because there is spirituality down and spirituality up. So this is rested. There is spirituality on the mountain top and there is spirituality in the lakes and rivers, etc. One thing you can be assured of is that what scripture is pointing or referring to is not nonsense. It is always fact about the nature of human beings. It is no guesswork. It is not nonsense. If it were nonsense Satan would have proven he could come out openly and show it is nonsense. They would have gotten rid of all the scriptures if they could be proven to be nonsense. They cannot be proven to be nonsense. It is deep, great knowledge.

9

The Destined Ethical World

The time of the global community has arrived and even though a super power like the United States of America has really the power to enforce its will or punish people so severely with its superior arms of weaponry, good sense intelligence tells our leaders in America, that that would be, in the long run, a suicide effort and that it's best to invite people to come together and help shape or form an authority that will represent all nations, all communities, all people.

The Destined Ethical World

Human beginning is given in the Bible in Genesis and that beginning is the Garden of Eden. The Garden of Eden is another way of saying Paradise and in the Qur'an it's also called, the Garden. But the picture that we get in our minds, or that is given to our minds when we read the Qur'an about the beginning of human existence, is an existence that was in heaven above. Many people think in heaven there are only angels; G_d, angels and good people. But this picture begins with G_d's plan to put a man on earth and give human beings responsibility for the environment that they find themselves in and that means the total environment, where ever the place is. But eventually human beings will be invited by circumstances after G_d invites them, firstly, to see the whole earth as the environment for their life aspirations and livelihoods; and not only the whole earth, but also the skies. This is the way it is presented in our religion, in the Qur'an.

Human beginning in Garden of Eden

If we understand it as students of the Bible, and I am, I think, a very blessed student of the Bible. I spent many hours and years studying it. If we understand the Bible, it is saying the same thing; that man's beginning started in heaven, and the same one makes trouble for the heaven that's presented in the Qur'an or in the sacred book of the Muslims; a heaven where the enemy of humanity comes into the picture as soon as he's informed or learns that the Creator, G_d, is going to make human beings responsible for the environment. He is the enemy of humanity called, Satan in Christian society, and Shaitan in Muslim society. The same one appears in heaven before man is established in the earth and he rejects G_d's plan to establish humans as the ones to be responsible for the environment on earth. He rejects that.

A Paradise map to global leadership

With that said, we want to focus now on space as environment and doing this with hopes of better understanding what the Paradise is; what the Eden, or the Garden of Paradise is. Eden is Paradise, but Eden is also a Paradise map to global leadership; the destined ethical world society that our learned leaders are working hard to advance, or to get more support for; a global ethical society on this planet earth.

Ethics can be traced to the effort to arrive at what is ethical. It's traced back to the moral urges, the good moral urges in the soul of people, or man. Governance and global trends are driven by consumerism, love of wealth, love of comforts, material comforts, etc., and ethics. It is driven by both consumerism and ethics. Both religious and secular institutions are contributing to the forming of an ethical world order, or an ethical world society.

The time of the global community has arrived

Eden as a message speaking to all of man's major aspirations speaks to the issues confronting the world at this present time and all of these issues are manifesting themselves in light of what the new reality is. And the new reality for people on this planet earth is that the main focus or the main thing we should be looking at in order to understand what is influencing and shaping everything on earth for man is no longer our separate nations. I remember when only a few nations were so powerful that they were determining the issues and the future, really, for all the other nations. And the United States of America has survived the competition to become the one out front world leader. But not even the United States of America is in any position or situation to lead the world, alone.

The time of the global community has arrived and even though a super power like the United States of America has really the power to enforce its will or punish people so severely with its superior arms of weaponry, good sense intelligence tells our leaders in America, that that would be, in the long run, a suicide effort and that it's best to invite people to come together and help shape or form an authority that will represent all nations, all communities, all people.

And that authority should be rooted in moral innocence, in moral life excellence. That authority should want to bring about the authority of morally responsible government for all people, for all nations. So, I repeat, Eden as a message is speaking to all of man's major aspirations; speaking to the issues confronting the world at this present time, a time of globalization.

The Destined Ethical World

Sacred scripture presents the skies and the earth, the universe and calls all of this that is put into focus a resource field for human interest. Now when we read in Genesis how G_d says that the world was void, empty, it means nothing there. And from nothing G_d caused, in human beings, the spirit to move out and search the darkness. And because man's spirit moved away from his selfishness, away from his self-centered interests, outwardly, to search the darkness, to search what he did not know in his total environment, the world environment, G_d said let there be light where there's darkness in the deep; and there was light. This is Genesis in the Bible.

The darkness and the light

And in the Qur'an it says, "Then G_d created the darkness and the light". He created what we could not know before, what we could not understand before, what we could not approach and utilize before. He created that and that was in our way, because it was impeding our ability to progress our intelligence and improve our environment. So G_d actually created humans to meet that task and make progress. It all began with a spirit and if you have a spirit for understanding and you hold it, you're going to get an understanding, sooner or later. If you have a spirit for obedience to G_d and you hold it, you're going to be obedient sooner or later. But the moment you change your spirit, or let go your direction for your life, it's all over.

Another way of referring to human intelligence is to use the expression, common sense. Common sense, that's where it all began. We cannot go anywhere with our brains or with our sense, or with our intelligence, without using our five senses...That's how all knowledge is found and developed to grow into the higher knowledge we call the exact sciences. There is no way to get there except upon respect for common sense, respect for the five senses that ties us all together as intelligent beings.

Object reasoning won sway over moral urges

Scripture's most critical message offered to man for avoiding unnecessary crisis comes as a moral life condition warning man. Man is urged to protect his intelligence. This can be achieved if man chooses to keep his five senses in a morally innocent environmental plan, or the garden, the Paradise, the Eden concept.

Man in scripture represents an overriding moral strategy for safeguarding the social community and all of its necessary features. Hence, ultimately, destiny concerns moral life and industrial life ingenuity that gives us all these material things that we see and enjoy and recognize as progress on earth for human conditions on this planet earth. The story of humans in a community setting, starting with life on earth in a Paradise, given the name, Eden, serves to assist man; that is, industrial man, working man, for avoiding and explaining crisis. It all got started when object-reasoning won sway over moral urges, or moral urgings, in the human soul.

The serpent, or snake, charmed "Adam", into accepting to rationalize moral issues that were in the way of man's path to world leadership, and world dominance. Did the snake do this with man's interest in front of him? No, he did it with his own interest in front of him. In other words, the serpent, or Satan, would never help humanity rise to world power, or to world leadership. Moral design supported by cosmology (from cosmos) and universal logic were sacrificed to free "intelligent design". That's a relatively new expression, "intelligent design". This strategy was contrived by Satan; hence, "humanism", and "secularism" developed in time.

Satan is an open enemy not a mystery

These two (secularism and humanism) developed in time as a result of the scheming, or planning and plotting by the Satan, Shaitan. Some can't follow me too well because they think Satan is a mystery. Our scripture says Satan is your plain enemy, your open enemy. He's no mystery. He is not hidden. But you don't find him by looking for a person, race, or a particular color. You find him by looking for evil that is oppressing the humanity of mankind. And when you find that evil and find who supports it more than others, most likely you have identified the plurality of the devil. And he's not in one people. He's helped by everybody that wants to benefit from his strategy that they believe in, because they think this is the way to become the rulers on earth.

The Destined Ethical World

Adam is world leadership

Satan disguised as the serpent, charms world leadership. Now you understand more of what Adam represents. Adam represents world leadership. He (Satan) charms world leadership into serving his plan, as opposed to the creation plan. G_d made the universe to give us the plan for our advancement. How can I speak with such confidence, that I am representing the scripture or the revelation that comes from G_d? Our father Abraham, Ibrahim, in Qur'anic Arabic, when he was threatened by the ruler, who was a dictator (one of the oppressive Pharaohs of Egypt) and wanted to dominate all other nations and people on the planet earth, Abraham replied to his threats by saying, "The One who created me, will guide me."

Now scholars who search for G_d's meaning, not for the meaning that may satisfies me, but the scholars that search for G_d's meaning in what He says, they came to the conclusion that G_d is saying, "I made the world as a map. I made the world as a plan to guide you to all the things you need for your existence and for your progress and prosperity."

Studying G_d's creation, studying G_d's works, the old Prophets, called seers, came to the conclusion that there is a G_d, that there is a superior behind all this. And they called everything that made them marvel and wonder and so happy to discover, they called those things they viewed, and discovered, the handiworks of G_d. And it is so beautiful to recognize the great design that G_d put on things to guide man to the best possible future we can have in this creation.

Moral design sacrificed to free intelligent design

Moral design supported by cosmology and universal logic, was sacrificed to free intelligent design. This strategy, intelligent design, that is, was contrived by Satan, hence, humanism and secularism developed in time. Humanism and secularism have hurt the human community. Both have really hurt the human community, even though great progress has been made for education, and science, in a world divided, part of it religious and the other part secular.

Thoughts for Searchers

I repeat, these two developments have really hurt humanity and have held us back from the glorious future that G_d planned creation to give us. Satan disguised as a serpent, charms world leadership into serving his plan, as opposed to the creation plan. And not wanting to appear to be rude, and condescending, Satan very gingerly tells man, "Your moral innocence is stupid". A casual look into western psychology's evaluation of the human soul, and its intelligence bears out, what is here said. Keeping our five senses in moral life begins where a male and a female decide to make their home for themselves and for their children.

A picture to open our eyes

This is the message of Eden. It's a concept. It's a picture, not to be taken as something that existed before the world was or before human history started; but mainly as something that is given to us as a picture to open our eyes to what's going to transpire to prevent man from coming into the life that G_d created for man. Satan wants to keep us in the dark as to what G_d wants for our life. This interest has to be presented for their protection in their work environment. So we start in the home, needing an environment serving our life and needs as the Genesis picture or concept was intended to serve the first human, or the first man, or the first human community's life and progress.

Promised Land is promised opportunity

Lastly, moral interest, expresses itself as ethics, serving the last leg of progress as expressed as an ethical world society. So if we began in Eden, in Paradise, before man's life is described on earth, it's just describing an urge that is in man's soul. And that's really a great philosophical picture there that says everything that man can bring about on earth, representing his intelligence is nothing but an expression or an outgrowth of the urges in his soul. It all starts in the human soul. And it is expressed in the mind, or by the intelligence, and it succeeds only if it consults the true and innocent urgings of the human heart.

So the Promised Land is more than just a place or a piece of geography. Most importantly it is the land for us, mentally, the promised opportunity to use our minds and benefit from the production of our tools we call the mental tools. Abraham is a sign of that. In Qur'anic Arabic it is, "Millati Ibraheema Haneefah," translated, "The order of Abraham, the upright in his nature."

The Far Horizon

We return now to an earlier topic. We had the bow and we had the string and arrow. We said one was human spirit and one was G_d's Spirit, the Holy Spirit. The Qur'an gives you a mental picture of this. It says two arrows fired from the same bow. The arrows would be perfectly parallel, perfectly straight and they are fired from this single bow.

The arrows are fired by the string that is tightened. A lot of stress is put on the string. So this string fires both arrows. Did that come in the Qur'an from Muhammed in his time? No, it is also in the Bible. Joseph is a bow by a well. These are the exact words. So a bow is mentioned in the Bible, too, and it calls the human being a bow. The wood represents the stick that you bend. The power comes from the stick. You bend the stick but it wants to get back like it was. You are pulling, straining it, making it bend more and it wants to go back where it was. That is where the power comes from. It wants to get back where it was.

String of the bow represents potential

The string is pulled back. You are putting tension on the string, pushing the bow forward and pulling the string back. So there is tension on the bow and tension on the string. The bow enables the string to fire when you let it go. The bow will pop back where it was. It throws the string back where it was. And in doing so it fires the arrow forward, right?

The string belongs to the bow. So the bow and the string are the human being and the string represents potential and capacity. So the spirit strains for understanding or thirsts for understanding. It is the human spirit. It is my spirit and your spirit. The bow is a picture of how it strains for understanding. You pull on the string. You are straining the spirit and the human nature can only take so much.

Thoughts for Searchers

Straining the spirit

You have human nature in your left hand. That is the stick. You have the stick and you are straining the spirit. The stick is your body, your flesh, your mortal life. You are straining your spirit and sometimes that strain pops, breaks. It is too much for the mortal life. What you wanted is too much for the mortal life. So the string will break. You are straining the spirit. You are pulling it back and then you release them and when you release them you are firing two arrows.

Potential in human nature strains for understanding

Arrows show direction. They are going in a direction and they are going to a target. In the Qur'an it says, "The distant horizon, or the far horizon." So they are going to a faraway place, a definite place, far away. What is this saying? It is saying that is human nature and capacity, the potential in the human nature and capacity strain to get understanding. It will fire both the human spirit and the spirit of G_d. They will be fired from that body. The human spirit and the spirit of G_d will be fired from that body by straining what is human.

Straining to be in accord with G_d's Spirit

The string is human. The wood is human. The pole and the string they are human. By straining that, the purpose in the human capacity for understanding will be realized and when it's realized it is not just man's spirit. It is also G_d's spirit in man. If we want to ignite, or bring G_d's spirit into us, we have to ignite the human spirit, strain the human spirit. And when the human spirit is fired, G_d's spirit will also be with the human spirit. G_d's spirit accompanies the human spirit when the human spirit strains for what is right. When you are straining for what is right for human life and human purpose you are in accord with the Will of G_d. You are already in accord with the Will of G_d. So His Spirit will be with your spirit. That is all it is saying. G_d's Spirit will be with your spirit. It won't be just you a human. You will have both you and G_d working together. Muhammed, the Prophet said the person can strain to be so obedient to G_d that he comes so close in his obedience to G_d that if he will strike you, it is as though G_d struck you. G_d will be in him and G_d will be with his actions. When he does things it is just as though G_d did it.

The Destined Ethical World

Working in accord with G_d's purpose

There is the Qur'anic verse, "Yaa ay-yuhan nafsul mutma-innah, irji'e e-laa rab-biki raadeeyatam mardeeyah," translated, "return to your Lord pleased and pleasing." It means pleasing yourself and you're pleasing before your G_d. He is pleased with you, too. What is that saying? The key is to work for the excellence of human nature, for the excellent future and destiny of human beings on this planet. When you work for that you are working in accord with what G_d's purpose is for you being on this earth. You are in accordance with His Will. And if you do that He is going to be with you. His spirit is also in your spirit. Your human spirit is there and G_d's spirit is with you. G_d's spirit is in your spirit.

How did it get there? Did something happen up in the sky and He breathed it down here? No, you got in accord with the best of your nature. When you got in accord with the best of your nature you were in accord with G_d's Will and purpose for you. They both are the same. That is what it is saying.

The effort to please yourself in the right way that you are made to please it is the way that G_d wants you to act. So when that happens you are acting in accord with the Will of G_d and your human spirit is also G_d's Will and Spirit. G_d has no spirit like we have. G_d's Purpose and Will is your human spirit. Your human spirit has become G_d's Purpose and Will. So it is still human, but at the same time it is divine.

The far Horizon

It says the far horizon. That means the distant purpose, or as the Bible would say the destiny. Abraham was shown the destiny and Moses came behind him to lead the people to the destiny, into the Promised Land. The Far Horizon is the same as the destiny, or the Promised Land for the Christian, not for us. We have a different language. Where are you going? At that time maybe they were facing Jerusalem. I don't know. I can't say. They could have been facing Mecca, the Ka'bah. Now we know we face the Ka'bah and were doing that in the time of Muhammed, the Prophet.

Thoughts for Searchers

The human destiny

We're facing the Ka'bah. Now if the two arrows were shot, like the fingers from the body in tashahhud, if they were shot towards the Ka'bah, then what does the Ka'bah symbolize as our destiny? Is the Ka'bah our destiny? Yes, it is a symbol of our destiny. What is that destiny? The destiny is one human family under G_d, no superiority of race, color or anything else, no superiority of sex. The woman can pray by herself. She can pray in front of you. She doesn't have to have an imam to lead her in prayers at the Ka'bah. The human destiny is the Promised Land, not America. America can be the human destiny for a while and then turn out to be a fecal house.

So as long as we keep the human purpose, then America is the destiny, too. But if we lose the human purpose for human beings here under G_d then this is no more the destiny. I like to say our land is a portable land. We can carry it in our suitcase. Anytime it doesn't look right here we pick up our suitcase and go and sit it down somewhere else. But thank G_d we are in good shape. Now we can live here. If I were going to travel it would have been a long time ago. I would look like a fool traveling now. Everything I was asking for, it has come to pass. I can go out of here and not feel that the Klan is going to catch me and string me up on a tree. I can run for the presidency of the United States and I don't have to have any more fear than a white man. If they don't want him they are going to shoot him, too.

G_d inside of you more than anywhere else

Believe that G_d, Allah, is everywhere and believe that for human beings, for our interest in our life and in the world, G_d is more in us than He is anywhere else. G_d is more inside you right now more than He is anywhere else. Why should He be up in the moon or somewhere, or in some star out there far away from me and He is there for me? No, if He is somewhere for me He should be right here. And that is where he is, right here inside of us, when we become obedient in His will and enjoy it; not just obedient, you have to enjoy it, it's your pleasure. That is why it says (in Qur'an), "Oh soul pleased." It has to be your pleasure.

The Destined Ethical World

Spirit of G_d hovers like a bird

When it is your pleasure to be with G_d and to have Him near you, close to you like that, you will then know the presence of G_d. You won't doubt it. And you will know that G_d is in you. G_d is in you and yet as far away from you as the farthest star in the universe; at the same time as close to you, as Allah says in the Qur'an, "As your jugular vein." He's as close to you as your artery, your life vessel that takes the blood from your heart to your body and keeps it alive. He is that close, but at the same time as far from you as the farthest imaginable thing in the universe.

The Spirit of G_d hovers. The Qur'an gives the picture or puts in the mind the picture of a bird or a flying thing. It says He hovers between a mortal and his heart. The mortal means his fear for his own life and what his heart wants. Your heart wants to be good but your fear of your own life sometimes holds you back from doing all of the good you can do or from being as good as you can be. So it says G_d is between the two. Your heart wants something and your mortal life wants something. It wants food, clothing, shelter, sex and fun, but my hearts wants to please my G_d or it wants me to be an upright, decent person.

G_d not in me as either extreme

G_d is not in me in the extreme where I want to be a perfect person. And He is not in the extreme where I'm fearing for my mortal life and I'm afraid that I won't be happy if I do all of these things I will be short changed. I can only go so far to the other extreme because I want to keep so much of this physical thing going, the fun life or whatever. G_d is not in either extreme. That is what it is saying. He is right in the middle. What is that saying? G_d, He does not need to go to heaven. You need to go to heaven and G_d certainly is not in hell and is not going to help you go to hell.

You do not have to be perfect to please G_d

So G_d is not in either extreme and He's there to bring you to the "golden mead," a happy medium as we say as an expression. G_d wants you to come to that happy medium. I think that is a good expression because we are talking about being pleased and pleasing our G_d. G_d wants you to come to that happy medium where you are not in the far extreme where you fear the lie you told is going to cause you to be killed, or it is going to put you in hell; and you are striving not to tell any lie, ever, and you think that is going to get you into heaven. That is the minimum you need to do, thinking, "I can't get into heaven if I tell a lie."

G_d is between the two extremes and He hopes to bring you to see that to please Him you don't have to be perfect. He didn't create you to be perfect. He made angels to be perfect. He made human beings to be fated to trial and error until they get guidance and then to follow guidance as much as they can. Isn't that what Allah says? He says, "Do as much as you can of it."

This is a loving G_d. This is not a G_d Who has no love for you. He is a G_d Who has great love for all human beings and all of the things He created. So He loves you and if you tell a little lie, you put yourself in hell. G_d is not going to put you in hell.

10

The Continued Life of the Human Soul

I thank Allah for this existence that He has blessed us to share. It is a blessing. And the route that we were put on didn't start with Muslims acknowledging the religion or acknowledging Allah and the Qur'an. It started with the first soul on this continent who found itself at a lost to understand circumstances that it was put in. And it started reaching outwardly without even scripture to guide it to the name of G_d or anything. It started reaching outwardly, crying to the distances, "I know there is a just G_d. I know there is justice somewhere out there."

Thoughts for Searchers

Al-Islam wants communities established on earth that are in accord with the Will and guidance of G_d; not one nation, communities, nations, plural, more than one. G_d wants us to establish many community models throughout society as a life pattern or picture for the ideal society. So this is the biggest task that we have as Muslims, to use our brain, our thinking people, the best of our thinking people, male and female. We are to use our brain to imagine a bigger, better and more productive environment for human beings to live in. And we are to work together for that, to realize that, to see that materialize. We're to have a select number of leaders working for that all the time, devoted and working for that all the time.

The universal law

G_d wants us to establish our self in community. That's the universal law. No human being, no single member of society can establish him or herself, except in community life. You can't have your career. You can't have your great future to yourself. It's impossible. That's not reality. You can only have it in community life. So we have to select a community life that we identify with and love and feel comfortable with and want to invest in. We want to invest our whole life in and we want to establish our contributions in that community for ourselves, for personal benefit, for the benefit of our wives, our mates and for the benefit of our children to come, for generations. That's what we have to do. This is the plan of the planners who live and abide when everything else has gone. All nations and civilized efforts will deteriorate and will go from the earth like dust taken by the wind. But those who plant themselves in G_d's Plan and then work it in the earth to establish that as a reality, they abide forever, for as long as the earth abides.

For as long as the earth abides

This effort of mine, you think it's just for now or just for your children to come? Do you think it's just for the year 2000 or 3000? No, this is for as long as the earth abides. If something should happen on this continent to make it impossible for human beings to live here, if you have my spirit, you will be with those who leave this continent and go to a place to restart their life all over again. So we have to establish self in community. The first community to establish our self in is the Muslim community, because we identify as Muslims. Then, we have to establish the Muslim community in the Christian community, in Christian America. And I have worked hard to show you how this can be done safely; not only safely but with the help and support of our Christian neighbors. G_d has guided me to that.

Go as in a race

We have to do it in partnership with other faith communities and that's what G_d means when he says to us, "Go as in a race after all that is good". He means the Muslims should go as in competition with good Christians, good Jews, good others, but only after the things approved by G_d. We will be competing with them for things that are halal (permissible) for Muslims and that's money, etc. Did you think money was haram (forbidden)? Look, if that's you, if you're going to hold to that decision, please exclude me from your life, your conversation, your memory. Take me out of your memory, please.

The free under G_d

This is the great season for the free under G_d. So we want to have alliances with the best of the people from Christianity and other religions; and certainly Christianity, more importantly, because most of us come from Christian families and with government itself. Government has been conceived for us on this continent, citizens of the United States, by men who were aiming for the best and most just form of government, the founding fathers. Their intent was so pure and good that G_d has caused this nation to survive while others have died and been destroyed.

He has caused this nation to stand strong while others have been trembling and shaking and dropping off their leaders and not succeeding in this world. He has caused this nation to be the leader, the leading political body on this planet. That's a fact whether we like it or not, whether we like ugly America or not. I don't like it either. I like beautiful America. I don't like ugly America. I'm with you there. But I'm going forward with America, because I love beautiful America. Oh brother, I'm going to kiss her all the way down to the finish line, beautiful America. You don't like it? You don't have to like it. Lump it, pump it, whatever you want to do with it. You aren't going to deprive me of my blessings. I know what Allah has blessed me with and you aren't going to take any of them away. I am very selfish when it comes to giving up my blessings.

So we have to do this in partnership with good government, with the good religious establishment, firstly; then with good government and also with good business establishment. So let us go home, all the way to the finish line. Let us have "jannatain", two Paradises, and let us not give up our share that G_d created us for of this world.

The Day of Religion

This is the Day of Religion. Never has this happened before that Christian leaders with authority in Christian doctrine and Muslim leaders and Jewish leaders come together to find accord that enables them to speak with one voice to the audience to help the audience appreciate G_d more in their life; to appreciate faith more in their life; to go back home and be a better faith person; if not a Muslim be a better faith person; if not a Christian be a better faith person; if not a Jew be a better faith person; if not a Buddhist be a better faith person.

So this is what is happening. This is the Day of Religion. Now in the Day of Religion what should we expect? This is the Day of Religion on earth according to my perception of the time and what is happening. This right now, in this month, in this time right now, is the Day of Religion, on this earth, on the whole globe. This is my perception. Now, if I am correct, what should Muslims expect? G_d says, "And I have preferred for you Al Islam as religion". We should expect Al Islam to have its most glorious time on this earth in the very near future. So let us ask G_d for guidance, forgiveness, first.

The Judgment is here

The Qur'an points us to a time that is called the day when everything will be concluded. All of our doubts and suspicions, all of our aspirations, etc., will be concluded. It is when man will have a situation to be in touch with man all over the planet earth; a one world system of communication. We have it now. So now if we propagate the religion the whole world can get it if we are free to propagate it. Never did that happen before. So you want to know when the

Judgment is coming? It is here! You want to know when the Day of Religion is? It is now! You want to know when is the Great Standing? It is now! The Great Meeting is now. Someone may say, "No, that is after the earth and everything is destroyed." Well, it already has been destroyed and it has appeared again. Do you think the physical world is going to be destroyed? G_d made the physical world. Why would He destroy this physical world that He made, for what? The world is not sinning, we are sinning on it. I'm the son of Elijah Mohammed, reborn.

We have to come together

Aren't we silly if we don't see a connection for ourselves as people of faith, when we know the same G_d that brought about the community of one brought about the community of the others? We have to come together. We can't afford any longer to ignore and not acknowledge each other. We have to acknowledge each other. This world has become too small. This earth is too small, too populated, too many of us on it, too crowded. I have to share that walkway with a Christian and a Christian has to share the walkway with me and with a Jew and with a Buddhist. The world has just become too small for us to avoid each other and never see each other for a life time. We're going to see each other every day and we have to share this gift of the planet earth. That's what it is. It's a gift. It's a trust to us. G_d gives it to us as a trust.

We're going to have to share this planet earth with each other and if we expect to fare well in the future we're going to have to not only accept each other, we're going to have to find ways to work together for a better earth for all of us. And that's what G_d wants. We'll never convert each other. The Christians will never convert all people to Christianity. The Jews will never convert all people to Judaism and they don't even want to. And the Muslim will never convert all people to Islam. We'll never do that. G_d never told us to do that.

Though religion has been the world's biggest oppressor, the Qur'an says religion's merits are more than the demerits. The Qur'an's fresh air way of addressing prophetic "End of Time", is intended for the sharpening of human perception; perception in the intellect regarding the history of religion how, in one hand, religion has been offering charity and giving charity, and in the other, religion has been greedy for power, even over nations. Therefore, it is important to be conscious of the fact that some scriptures clumsily fabricate a message bearing cloth as a strategy for survival and also as a strategy for war. These strategic planners, in planning the death of brutal, savage governments, also, subtly plan a peace times and a time for discarding their cloth stained with bad blood. Rising spiritual and social dynamics, rising public awareness and literacy in the public, rising respect in government for the value of the common citizens in their publics, honoring the equal rights of the common citizen in the life of the state, all of such makes understandable the prophetic Qur'anic expression, Day of Religion.

The table of ethics and global rule

In the Qur'an, the expression Day of Judgment is the same as Day of Religion. Of sacred scripture, the Qur'an's words read: "None can touch it," meaning none can reach its insights but the purified ones. None can touch it but the purified ones". Most of man's Holy Scriptures are arduous fitness exercises in moral leadership training. Engagers who remain constantly devoted will grow in moral firmness to qualify for a seat at the table of ethics and global rule or order.

So the words of G_d in scripture are intended to produce a very special leadership for the world. But you have to go through arduous training. In world religions, the student will find the most disturbing reading, on first sight, when you start to read the scriptures. If you are morally sensitive and curious, you are going to find the reading of scripture very disturbing on first reading. And on second sight, you are going to perceive the most intriguing and productive literary fabrication. You are going to be amazed and you will say, "Oh, this is the most productive literary fabrication I have ever experienced or read!" Hence, the Qur'an's first word in its revealing itself to our Prophet Muhammed, the prayers and the peace be on him, is "Read!" This word, "Read," is prophetic, having to do with old prophecies. Reading can be mentally, morally, intellectually and spiritually liberating. However, the benefits are expected to only be opened for the constantly devoted student. Regarding using our five senses, they are necessary if we are to gain any knowledge or information. Knowledge and information must come through the five senses. I know perhaps you are thinking that knowledge is intuitive. That is true. But if you don't use your five senses and work those senses very diligently and constantly, there will be no true intuitive knowledge. In fact, some authorities on the psychology of man say that really the sixth sense that we come to understand - intuition or inspiration - is all the senses in one. It is the power of the five senses producing one sense or one medium - intuition.

Brothers and sisters in the family of human beings

I call it the Day of Religion because for the first time in the history of the great religious communities of Judaism, Christianity and Al Islam, we are becoming brothers and sisters in the family of human beings. We have representatives meeting with each other, representatives from Judaism, representatives from Christianity, and Al Islam, meeting with each other and discussing the global situation for us all; offering our support to each other and asking each other for help to write and form an agenda that we all can support so that we will serve the interest of not just ourselves as a religious group of representatives, but ourselves as human beings. How can we behave in the world? How can we communicate to the world so that we contribute to the better life and better conditions of people here and everywhere? That is what we want.

We're now on a level plane

For the first time, we have great religions coming together with the interest of human life, the one life, at heart and willing not to just tolerate each other saying, "I know my religion is not the only religion recognized by G_d. This is a free society. I grant you your right to have your own religion." No, we're not coming from that arrogance. We're not coming from that high place towering over somebody else and speaking down to each other. We're on the level plane. We respect each other as brothers and sisters. We respect the religions as having the same importance, because if your religion is your religion it is just as serious in your heart as mine is in my heart and we have to respect that. We have to respect each other, care about each other and not just tolerate differences, but support each other in our differences.

Help him to be what he says he is

Wouldn't it be better for us to support a member of our neighborhood who is a Christian, not a Muslim, support him in his religion if he's ignorant of his religion and we know his religion should be better represented in him than it is and we know about his religion? Shouldn't we tell him something from his holy book, from his Bible, to remind him, to make him more competent? Shouldn't we let him know that we have more respect than that for what he claims to believe and maybe he should know the value of his own religion? In the long run we would be helping to save the neighborhood, wouldn't we? But if we say, "He's a Christian and not worth anything. He's just disgraceful." You have no desire to help him, or you say, "He should be a Muslim." No, he shouldn't. You are taking a big chance. Help him to be what he says he is. He says he is a Christian, help him to be a Christian and once he is a good Christian, if he wants to become a Muslim it is a little bit safer.

The Christ Formula

Mr. W. D. Fard said to the United States government, "Give me these people who are dissatisfied with you and not content to be American black citizens. They are defying that. They want to be their own independent people, so let me take them out of your hair".

He did not design any new plan for himself or anything. He saw the plan in the Bible, Christ Jesus... You see he understood Christ Jesus in the Bible and he understood what it meant. He understood the formula. It is a formula for bringing about a certain effect. To convert people and eventually bring them back to their originality, that is the plan. But Christianity is so complicated that most Christians cannot get the benefit. But Mr. Fard proved that it works because he produced me. He set the stage to produce me and this is real. So it is a formula.

It is no new thing

The Christ formula has existed even before Christ. It is no new thing. The New Testament introduces it, anew, but it was not just in the Bible. It was in different parts of the world. They have this secret knowledge of how to put or make sure that the child is born in an environment that is sincere and obedient to G_d, whatever they call the G_d. And then it is designed to condition his mind to be independent so that he thinks independently and is given support from the members, whatever the congregation is. Whatever the congregation is, give him support from the best of the members and as he grows older this influence takes him over. Eventually, he comes to realize that he cannot fulfill his soul's needs without following that pattern that they set for him, or without living in that pattern and proceeding with his life upon that pattern. So it works. Where the other members are accepting things on face value he is not. He is conditioned not to accept things on face value.

It does not always work

They are trying to produce a leader who will be of and in that purity. And it works, but it does not work all the time. And that is why Jesus is named, Esaa, from the Arabic verb, asaa, meaning, "maybe", which alludes to, "perhaps". It does not happen all of the time. And that is why before Zachariah, they threw lots first. It means it was chance. Then they gave the child into the charge of Zachariah. Zachariah is a play on purity. Put him in the charge of purity so he wouldn't be defiled.

In the word "Esaa" are the Arabic letters Ain, Seen and then the letter, Ya. "Asaa" is the letters Ain, S and Y, but you pronounce it, "Asaa"; the same letters and you put the kasrah under the letter Ain and it becomes Esaa. That is his name. The root meaning hasn't changed. So that nature is in all of us.

The Wall Ace

You have heard of orphans as inheritors of what is under a wall (Qur'an) and the wise man (and Moses) came to the wall. He recognized that the inheritance was under that wall. So, he would not tear it down. And my name is Wallace (Wall Ace) and that was not accidental. The inheritance was supposed to be for the orphans, for the ones who didn't have parents to take care of them and oversee their life to see that they had what G_d established to be given to all human beings. There was nobody to take care of that for them. So they were orphans. That's the Prophet and that's us as a people.

Thoughts for Searchers

All people of the earth are slaves

G_d says in the Qur'an that He opened up his (Muhammed) breast, the chest area, expanded it so that there would be more room there for the whole of mankind. It means his heart. He expanded his breast so there would be enough room for the whole of mankind inside his heart, or inside his breast; and relieved him from the burden which weighed down the khalifah. His back is symbolic of the khalifah in him which weighed down his back.

Now usually men carry burdens, heavy things, upon their back. So that is to give the picture of a poor person who is regarded, treated as a burden bearer. The world has weighed his back down like the donkey in scripture. So the world has weighed him down and what burdens his back, also, specifically for him in his life as a person in the history, is the strain on his mind to bring the message to his people in Arabia and also the world of the liberation of mankind; not one people; not one man, but the whole of humanity. So he's carrying the weight of that desire to bring liberation to the whole of the people on this earth, because they all were slaves to their masters, to personal interests, to ideologies. But once the universal message comes that has as its recipient the soul of mankind, all the people then he knew that the world would be much better off and on its way to the destiny.

The need in the human soul

So G_d had to first open his heart, expand the room in his heart to accommodate all people. That shows a progression for the prophet. It means he was so sincere, he wanted to help people. First he saw the misery of the Arabs and that's what sent him up to the cave to call on a Higher Reality. Now to go forth he had to have in his heart the whole of mankind, not just the Arabs. So when that was done it was taken off his back and he was found an orphan. The Qur'an says, "Didn't we find you an orphan straying, worrying about the Arabs? Didn't we find you straying thinking the Jewish accomplishment for the religious community in Jerusalem was where you should begin? You should begin at the site of the Ka'bah, the symbol that represents the full light for all mankind. Your nature is cheated, so didn't we find you groping? And we said now we're going to turn you to a qiblah that will please you." Well that need in his soul is typical of the need in the human soul, period.

Christ principle is human innocence

The Qur'an also says that the Prophet removed the yokes like oxen have. This is referring to the human being carrying burdens like a slave. But, it didn't name any particular people. It didn't say Arabs or blacks, because the whole of mankind was treated as slaves. And who enslaves them? Their own souls enslave them because their own souls have not been awakened to the purpose for which G_d created them.

So the Christ principle is human innocence and that is what you need to receive the light of G_d for all mankind, for no particular people. So the opening chapter in the Qur'an (al-Fatiha) addresses the mentality that focuses on itself and excludes the rest of mankind. It says, "In the name of G_d, Allah, the G_d, the Gracious, the Compassionate" or "the Merciful Benefactor, the Merciful Redeemer". Then it says, "The praise is due to G_d the Lord of all the worlds"; not the lord of Israel. This is sent to the man whose heart is open to the whole of mankind. And it is said of Jesus Christ, "In my father's house are many mansions." To add to that, "And He found you drooping, an orphan with your back burdened, weighed down, and He opened your chest to receive the whole of humanity…This is a new language. The real Lord is the Lord of all people, not just one people. So G_d was revealing to Muhammed, the Prophet, a new language for the world to be reformed and the Prophet himself was found an orphan.

One day the treasure is going to be found under the wall

In the earlier days of this country's industrial development in people's homes Christian language was expressed by wall paper, especially those who could afford it. The wall paper was the language of Christianity, which shows that they had some understanding that the wall that protects and holds in, the same wall separates and keeps out. One day the treasure is going to be found under those walls and then the separation will be just and the enclosures will be just. The connections will be everywhere. People will be connected all over the world though living in their separate habitats. That's the time right now. You can see it as plain as day.

To Free Every Human Being

As to what is happening today that has an effect on the global community, I know it was revealed to Prophet Muhammed, everything. But as to what happens in the sunnah (lifestyle and traditions) of Muhammed, that is for us to live and grow in. That is why he established both. He established the fard, the Qur'an, and the sunnah.

As for the Qur'an, it is complete and says everything that needs to be said about the global community, its nature and how it is going to be concluded. It is told so vividly clear in the Qur'an. But as for our human interactions and how we are to advance our life as human beings in the world but also in the cause of G_d affecting the world and also in the soul of man, for man's pleasures and for his enlightenment or understanding, that continues. That grows and continues to grow after the Prophet and that is his sunnah. His sunnah is to free every human being to have the best and biggest life possible for the human soul. That's his sunnah. That is why women are obligated to carry out his sunnah, just like we are. Even women, they have to carry out his sunnah.

The continued life of the human soul

The sunnah of Muhammed is the continued life of the human soul in the material world G_d made for it to feed it and support it. That's his sunnah, the Qur'an, it's revelation, revealing G_d's plan for the world and warning us against Iblis' plan for the world and telling us how it is going to be concluded; because G_d saw the end of Iblis, how far he could go. So it also reveals how this world is going to be concluded. And there are clear teachings in the Qur'an, right now, that's apply to this present time we're living in, right now; describing it. I cannot describe it better than what is in the Qur'an already.

The Continued Life of the Human Soul

The end of time

In time, you're going to see that coming from me because I am going to point you to what is in the Qur'an. This time, just what is happening right now, how man's own planning is going to get out of his own control, it is already in the Qur'an as plain as day; how Satan is going to carry out what he said he's going to carry out and reach the end of his power and ability. He's going to reach the end of it and he's going to be able to affect what he said he would on human life. The language is there and the reality in this world bears witness to what it says in the Qur'an. I mean it fits it perfectly. The description is perfect.

And how can this not be the end of time or the end of the time for the schemes of Satan? He said, "Spare me until the day that they are raised". Isn't that what he said? Well, he has been spared and the dead are being raised. So what can happen after this that will make us believe, "Oh no, this is not the Day of Judgment, this is not the conclusion of things?" What will happen later is the conclusion of things? What can happen later that would fit the scripture as perfectly as this that is happening now fits the scripture? Nothing, so this is the end of time. The end of time does not mean the end of time. There are two times. There is man's time and G_d's time.

"Really, I'm not a serious believer"

The Satan sold man on accepting Satan's time and he's been running this world by Satan's time and calling it man's time. But it's Satan's time, doing exactly what Satan said he would have the people, the world to do. He said, "All, except those who are committed to You, that are Your special devotees; all the rest I will get". And he's gotten them. He can't go any further with it. There is nothing else for him to do. Even those in the Church, they go to church, set up in the church and identify with the congregation, with the authority over the Church. They accept the authority over the Church; that is, G_d's revelation, the word of G_d and all that. But to seriously believe in G_d and faith in the religion with sincere faith or real faith, they don't have it; very few. There will be those supporting the Church with their money, but if you confront them with those beliefs, they will say, "Really, I'm not a serious believer." I have experienced it and I'm sure you have. I leave that to them.

Thoughts for Searchers

So really, most of the people who are supporting religion are not really themselves strong religious converts. They go there and pay their dues but they come out into their world. They leave their church, or place of worship, synagogue, mosque, too, masjid, too. They leave those places and they go back to their world. And their world is the world of man. It is man's world and man's world has been divided by Satan's schemes. Satan has been successful in planting his schemes in man's world. And his schemes have brought man's world to be weak, brought it to its end. It is really at its end right now. It can hardly produce a president.

An idea that is bigger

They are trying. Who do they have? Mr. Obama, he's the best they've got, in my opinion. Those others who come out they look very weak to me…The president has to be inspired. He has to really believe in something bigger than materialism or material realities. He has to believe in an idea that is bigger than all of that. He has to believe in G_d. He has to believe in humanity. He has to believe in tried ideas of philosophy, or ideologies that have made for the advancement of human life in a humane world. If he is not touched by things and idea and history like that he is not inspired. And he is going to be dead to the people who need life.

This world is in need of life, the real spiritual life in us. That is what we're needing more than anything else right now, because we have become void almost of that life, giving ourselves to the routine things that we have to do. And our time all occupied, because you cannot make you by yourself. You have your wife working, too. You cannot just work yourself…So Satan has brought us to this time, when his way of running the world is occupying our life to the maximum where there is little time for anybody to be alone with their soul to contemplate the realities of G_d's creation and to come into a mind to awake and absorb things from reality to become a special leader for the people. No, he will fix it so that the possibility of that happening is almost zero.

The Continued Life of the Human Soul

Signs of G_d plain today

The signs of G_d are just as big and plain while all of this is happening. We know what is happening. I know what is happening. These people have to wake up and they're going to wake up and start doing the things that they have to do to bring the world to accommodate the best of human life in its traditional values. They're going to have to do that. And it is going to mean bringing in a different kind of treatment of people. They're going to have to recognize good people, to prepare the world for good people. They're going to have to eliminate those that Satan has produced to bring our world down; and they do exist, behind the scenes. I believe in the very near future we're going to have better minds and better thinkers competing for the leadership in this country.

The focus is life itself

Three is very strong in the natural world. Roots, stems and branches that is the plant world, isn't it? In the Qur'an, our life is compared to a plant. It didn't say an animal. So what does that tell us about the three? The three is developmental. So the Jews, they were all about ten, conscience, enlightenment, and knowledge, etc. That was their fascination. It is still their fascination, but Allah did not choose that for us, the Muslims. He chose three for the Muslim congregation, not ten. You know W.E.B. Dubois and the talented tenth? It refers to education. It has all to do with education. Al-Islam does serve that but that is not the focus. The focus is life itself.

The Bible starts out with Adam, the first man, having two sons directly from him, Cain and Abel. One represents the cultivation or the development of the material world for business to supply for us our needs, industry, etc. That is Cain. The other one represents agriculture, farming, and the attention is on animal life. Abel was a herdsman and he took care of animals and animals have to eat from the land. So man first fed himself from the land, then, he got bigger. He had animals and he needed more land to feed his animals. He had a market. He had to sell to a big market. So the home life is Abel's life, family life and raising cattle and the industrial life is Cain's. He is the industrial life.

Thoughts for Searchers

Social life was swallowed by industrial life

So his slaying his brother doesn't mean he slew him outright. It means he took over his brother. He became the master, or he became the boss above his brother; which means industry eventually grows to be stronger than family life, even stronger than the farmer. The agricultural man eventually comes under industry, the industrial man.

He brings his social life to be swallowed by industrial life. Isn't that what happened to us? Isn't that what happened to family? Isn't that how this world is ending? Industrial life is swallowing up family life, social life. So developmental life is the focus. How is life developing? Is it still developing as a plant? Is it still rooted? Is it still growing from its roots and presenting itself in the sunlight and forming branches to balance itself in giving charity? Is it still doing that? That is our focus, the developmental life.

The Qur'an says you are caused to come through three veils of darkness. So that is the purpose of G_d, to bring us through these three stages; three stages that represent darkness and they are the material, rational and the spiritual. All of these are states of darkness until you come into the knowledge of the oneness and unity of G_d's creation and realize that Allah is Akbar (greater, more important). He is over everything. He is bigger than everything. He is more important than everything. Then you will bring your physical life to acknowledge G_d. You will bring your rational life to acknowledge G_d and you will bring your spiritual life to acknowledge G_d.

G_d made the world to show us ourselves

When the rational cannot take society any further they are left to their spirit. And we may not think spirit is higher than rational but it is, because fire can't burn without air. So those stars they're talking about out there, they are in a state of confusion. That is why they are still burning. They are going to have to, one day, come to rest. And when they rest they are going to be just like this. They are going to have their oxygen out there or their gases out there just like we have it on this planet that has rested. But they are just burning now. They cannot support life. They can only give their energies and support to the balance of the system and their energies reach us some kind of way, maybe. But as far as having life for themselves, no, they cannot support life. They are burning up. They burn up or burn out. Isn't that how some people are?

G_d made this world to show us ourselves. Some people are just like that, big headed, big minded, big brained, thinking they know everything. They cannot support life, but they can just burn up and show you how much they can burn. They can show us how big they are and how much they can burn, but can they support life? No, because they are all about themselves and their own intelligence. To support life they have to cool off. They have to cool off, first.

G_d Himself Teaches You

The Qur'an says, "It is Allah Who teaches you", plural, not singular. It can't be speaking to the Prophet. It is obvious that He spoke to the Prophet. Allah communicated to us through the Prophet, but it says it is Allah Who teaches you. So that means, yes, the Prophet teaches you. But if you deserve it, G_d will teach you. All the time it is G_d Who is teaching you, because the Qur'an is His word to all of us. And if you study sincerely you are going to be educated in the Qur'an without a teacher. All of us get guidance and all of us get better educated in Al Islam by reading and studying the Qur'an.

Qur'an is the imam

The Qur'an, its role is also to serve as our imam (leader). It says He revealed the book as an imam to the people of Moses. That is to tell us our book, too, is a man like unto Moses. So our Qur'an, too, is revealed to us to be our imam. You see, the movement of Al Islam in the Prophet is the liberation of mankind, all people. And what has prevented the people from being awakened to their best nature and the course they should take to freedom? It is religious leaders who keep the whole pot and give the people a little broth. That has been the problem.

No priesthood

So the Qur'an and Muhammed, the Prophet, come to make it available to everybody. And they don't have to come through anybody, no intercessor, no mediator, to mediate between G_d and you; no priesthood. That means our religion doesn't depend on religious or spiritual leaders to keep it in the public. Men and women are obligated to follow the sunnah (the traditions) of our Prophet where no one leads the other. You are to perform it independently, on your own. All of this points to the order that we need for mankind on earth to get rid of all forms of slavery, etc. So Prophet Muhammed is to be seen as a liberator, a teacher, who teaches universality, universals, and situates us to get the maximum benefit from academic studies or interests, education, etc.

Coming to the Right Perception

What we're trying to do and I think we're succeeding, is to free minds, condition minds to connect with the Qur'an, the language of the Qur'an; connect with it so they'll read not only the literary text, but they'll connect with the insights and I think it's coming. Yes, it's coming.

I didn't have any help like you all have and G_d blessed me to get it. The only help I had was faith in my own intelligence, faith in my rational mind, and faith in G_d. And G_d will not lead anyone astray. Now, G_d is definitely merciful and if anyone is led astray, that person will be redeemed by His Mercy. Yes, that's all the help I had. When you are taught to depend upon your own rational mind you aren't going to be blindly led. You're not going to be led blindly and you're not going to see that that conflicts with reason and not suspect that there is something wrong with it, either hidden singly, or it's just a lie.

The help I'm giving you all is the help that's in the Qur'an. But I'm giving it to you, plainly, and consciously, that you have to connect back with real life and real nature and the nature before man changed it and put his language to it. And that's a good situation to be in, in order to come to the right perception, or to get the Qur'anic insights.

The world not as dark now

The world is not as dark now as it was back there in his (Prophet Muhammed) day. It was much darker. Ignorance was heavier on the people in his day than it is nowadays. I was raised in a Christian country, in a Christian environment, in a church environment. I heard preachers preach. And I'm an African American born as the son of a man who had rejected the Church; my father, Elijah Mohammed. So I'm in that Christian environment. I'm hearing them preaching, but I already have been influenced to suspect that something is wrong with what they're saying. So I'm favored much more than Prophet Muhammed was. Yes, my circumstances favored me coming into the light much more than Prophet Muhammed's circumstances favored him coming into the light. If he had any advantage over me it was taken away by Mr. Fard when he said that this whole world is nothing but a lie. Everything is a lie.

We Will See Each Other Again

I thank Allah for this existence that He has blessed us to share. It is a blessing. And the route that we were put on didn't start with Muslims acknowledging the religion or acknowledging Allah and the Qur'an. It started with the first soul on this continent who found itself at a lost to understand circumstances that it was put in. And it started reaching outwardly without even scripture to guide it to the name of G_d or anything. It started reaching outwardly, crying to the distances, "I know there is a just G_d. I know there is justice somewhere out there."

That is where it started and that is still in us. If we awaken in that particular spirit and mind to understand, then Allah is with us. And we have awakened in that particular spirit and mind to understand. That is why Elijah Mohammed followed Mr. Fard away from Christian society and Christianity. And that is why his son, too, kept the same spirit and the same determination to understand, "Why am I in these circumstances?"

Soul never at a standstill

And I got the help of scripture, mainly Qur'an. I was not in the Bible. I started off in the Qur'an. And when I said we share the same existence, our existence can't be understood unless we understand what we have experienced as a people and more importantly, as a spirituality, as a sensitivity, as a soul of that people. They all share one sensitivity. They all share one spirituality that was formed by circumstances that they were touched by more than anybody else. So that made us a product or design after the influences or the circumstances in our history.

Thoughts for Searchers

That forming of us is more important than Wallace D. Mohammed or these different individuals. We only have big meaning once we put ourselves in that group experience and group history for the soul, mainly because many times the mind couldn't walk the path, couldn't even know what was happening, couldn't travel. It was at a standstill. But the soul is never at a standstill. It is always sensing and wanting to understand what it is sensing. That is our true life and that is the life that we don't have, alone. We have it only as a people.

We will see each other again, soon

Remember when I said that to get into heaven you can't go in by yourself? You have to go in as a community, a community as survivors of slavery. If we forget that, to me, we lose sight on what's real in our life and where we should be going. So, ensha Allah (G_d willing), we will see each other again, soon. I thank G_d for us.

Thoughts for Searchers

Glossary of Terms

Allah. The One and Only G_d.

Ayat. Arabic word meaning, "sign"; a verse in the Qur'an.

Bilal ibn Rabah. An Abyssinian slave who became a follower of Prophet Muhammed while still a slave. He was freed and eventually became a close companion of the Prophet, his treasurer, and the first caller to prayer in al-Islam.

Dikhr. Reflecting on G_d by reciting His names or attributes.

W. Fard Muhammed (W. D. Fard, Wallace D. Muhammed). The founder of the Lost Found Nation of Islam in the Wilderness of North America (Nation of Islam); the teacher of the Honorable Elijah Mohammed.

Al-Fatiha. The opening chapter of the Holy Qur'an.

G_d. In order to show due reverence to the name of G_d Almighty, we do not use any spelling that could in the reverse spell "dog".

Hadith. The reported sayings of Muhammed, the Prophet.

Halal. What is permissible in al-Islam.

The Honorable Elijah Mohammed. The leader of the Lost Found Nation of Islam in the Wilderness of North America (The Nation of Islam) from 1933-1975; the father of Imam W. Deen Mohammed.

Imam. In al-Islam, the leader of the group prayer.

Islam. More properly, al-Islam; the last of the monotheistic religions, established by Muhammed, the Prophet, a little more than 600 years after the time of Jesus Christ.

Jahiliyyah. Age of ignorance. The period of darkness and ignorance in Arabia before the Qur'an was revealed to Muhammed, the Prophet.

Jibril. Gabriel in Christian tradition; the angel or messenger of revelation.

Thoughts for Searchers

Jihad. Striving or struggling in the way of G_d.

Ka'bah. The house built by Ibraheem (Abraham) and his son, Isma'il (Ishmael), which is the orientation for Muslim prayer that is performed five times a day.

Miraj, or the Ascension. The spiritual ascension and journey of Prophet Muhammed to the 7 levels of heaven.

Muhammed, the Prophet. The last prophet of scripture who received the holy scriptures for Muslims, the Qur'an, over 23 years, and established the religion of Islam and the model Islamic community.

The Nation of Islam. More properly, the Lost Found Nation of Islam in the Wilderness of North America; the proto-Islamic movement founded in 1930 in Detroit, Michigan, by Mr. W. Fard Mohammed and was led by the Honorable Elijah Mohammed from 1933-1975.

Qiblah. The direction (towards the Ka'bah in Mecca) that the Muslim orientates himself to perform his/her salat (prayer) five times a day.

Qur'an. The word of G_d revealed to Muhammed, the Prophet, over a period of 23 years. It is the number one source of guidance for Muslims.

Salat. The formal prayer ritual in al-Islam. Salat requires the adherent to pray (in a group) five times a day at prescribed times.

Shaitan. The Qur'anic Arabic word for Satan, or the devil.

Sunnah. The lifestyle, sayings and traditions of Muhammed, the Prophet; the number two source of guidance for Muslims.

Tashahhud. The portion of salah (obligatory prayer) where the Muslim sits facing the Qibla (Ka'bah) in Mecca and points his/her right index finger in witness.

Wudu'. The ritual washing with pure water before salat (prayer).